# ASTONISHING APPLES

the orthern plate

The Northern Plate series celebrates the bounty of the Upper Midwest by focusing on a single ingredient, exploring its historical uses as well as culinary applications across a range of dishes.

Other books in the series:

*Homemade with Honey* by Sue Doeden

*Modern Maple* by Teresa Marrone

*Rhubarb Renaissance* by Kim Ode

*Smitten with Squash* by Amanda Kay Paa

*Sweet Corn Spectacular* by Marie Porter

 MINNESOTA
HISTORICAL
SOCIETY PRESS

# ASTONISHING
# APPLES

## JOAN DONATELLE

the Northern plate

www.mnhspress.org

The Minnesota Historical Society Press is a member of the Association of American University Presses.

Manufactured in [the United States of America/Canada]

10 9 8 7 6 5 4 3 2 1

♾ The paper used in this publication meets the minimum requirements of the American National Standard for Information Sciences—Permanence for Printed Library Materials, ANSI Z39.48-1984.

International Standard Book Number

ISBN: 978-0-87351-965-6 (paper)

**LIBRARY OF CONGRESS CATALOGING-IN-PUBLICATION DATA**
Donatelle, Joan.
Astonishing apples / Joan Donatelle.
  pages cm. — (Northern plate)
Includes index.
ISBN 978-0-87351-965-6 (pbk. : alk. paper)
1. Cooking (Apples) I. Title.

TX813.A6D66 2015
641.6'411—dc23

2015011483

..........................

*Astonishing Apples* was designed and set in type by Cathy Spengler. The typefaces are Chaparral, TheSans, and Brandon Printed.

Photograph on page 8 from MNHS collections.

Photographs on pages 54, 71, 75, 102–3, 137, and 141 by Joan Donatelle.

Photographs on pages 3, 12–13, 14, 26, 113, 151, and 167 by David L. Hansen, University of Minnesota.

*For my husband David,*
    *always present for encouragement and collaboration*

# CONTENTS

# ASTONISHING APPLES

# INTRODUCTION

One of my fondest memories is of my grandmother reaching up into her large apple tree with her special basket to snatch an apple for me. I remember the sun sparkling through the branches and the taste of the apple: crisp, tart, juicy, crunchy, sweet—pure happiness! In her cupboard there was always a stash of apple butter to be enjoyed on toast. When autumn arrived, so would the perfect apple pie, elevating Sunday dinner from simple to sublime.

Apples are one of the primal fruits to be enjoyed by humankind. Archaeologists have found remnants of charred apples in prehistoric Swiss dwellings that date back to 6500 BCE. Historically, the apple was prized in many ancient cultures; China, Greece, Rome, and Scandinavia all have apples in their history. Today, quality apples are grown around the world. The top producers are China, the United States, Turkey, Poland, and Italy.

The apple tree is a member of the rose family (Rosaceae). Scientists have traced its origins to Southeast Asia, to the area between the Caspian and Black Seas. The first ancient wild trees, crabapples, *Malus sieversii,* can still be found growing wild in that area. In 2010, in a project led by an Italian team in conjunction with Washington State, the apple genome was decoded. It was found that a single apple had 57,000 genes, the highest number for any plant studied up until that time.

The number of varieties of the domesticated apple tree, *Malus domestica,* is mind boggling: more than 7,500 grown around the world and more than 2,500 grown in the United States. When referring to different types of apples, the term *cultivar* is used. A cultivar is a plant variety produced by natural breeding for desirable characteristics. Apples in the Midwest, for example, are developed to be winter hardy. Other characteristics include taste, juiciness, texture, storage stability, and resistance to pests and fungus. With so many different cultivars, everyone can have their favorite. What's yours?

## APPLES: A SUPERFOOD AMONG US

We have all heard the saying, "an apple a day keeps the doctor away," but when folk wisdom is substantiated by hard scientific testing, I wonder: how did anyone ever make this discovery? When did someone eat an apple and say, "Wow, not only is this fruit delicious, but I feel better when I consume it, too"? One account credits the Welsh for coining this proverb, and not that long ago, perhaps as recently as 1860. The concept likely has been around for centuries because, as we know, the Romans and the Greeks had a fondness for apples. There is also evidence of the fruit's health benefits going back 1,500 years in the traditional Ayurvedic medicine of India.

A recent study from the University of Ohio published in *Medical News Today* showed a 40 percent lower level of substances that cause hardening of the arteries and a substantial reduction of the bad LDL cholesterol in apple eaters. Other health claims suggest that apples help

- avoid Alzheimer's disease
- protect against Parkinson's disease
- decrease the risk of diabetes
- prevent gallstones
- promote a healthier heart
- neutralize irritable bowel syndrome
- avert hemorrhoids
- treat diarrhea *and* constipation
- detoxify the liver
- boost immunity
- prevent cataracts

One primary reason for these many health benefits comes from apples' abundance of soluble dietary fiber. Apples are also a great source of vitamins C and B-complex, phytonutrients, minerals, calcium, potassium, phosphorus, phenolic compounds, flavonoids, and the antioxidant quercetin. So you see, there is a seed of truth that the apple can promote overall health. Grown all over the world, this fruit is a nutritional powerhouse, aka a superfood, and is nothing short of miraculous.

Please pass the apples.

## JOHNNY APPLESEED: FACT OR FICTION?

There actually was a Johnny Appleseed, but the real person was a bit different from the familiar cartoon version.

John Chapman was born in 1774 in Massachusetts. His father, Nathaniel, a farmer, was a minuteman during the Revolutionary War, fighting in the battle of Concord. His mother, Elizabeth, died in childbirth when his younger brother was born, leaving behind John and his older sister. His dad remarried four years later and had ten more children. When John was a young man, his father apprenticed him with a plant nursery.

Eventually, Chapman established commercial orchards in Pennsylvania and then the Ohio frontier. In the late 1700s, the settling of the Northwest Territory—what became Ohio and Indiana—was in full swing. The Ohio Company of Associates offered permanent homesteads of a hundred acres to settlers who planted a hundred apple trees. John Chapman arrived in advance of the settlers to clear the land and plant. The apples were really not good for eating out of hand; at most they could be used to produce hard cider or apple brandy. His work was not a helter-skelter flinging of seeds over the countryside, whistling and singing along the way. The land was cleared and planted, maintained and sold. Chapman would sell seedlings or use them to barter for other needed goods. At that time, seedlings cost the equivalent of about six cents.

Chapman was indeed an eccentric individual; despite his successful business, he was often seen wearing a pot on his head instead of a hat, his clothes shabby, his feet bare. He was a loner and loved nature. He followed the new faith of the Church of Swedenborg, spreading his beliefs wherever he traveled and planted, preaching to Native Americans as well as settlers. Chapman never married, believing that practicing abstinence would help him get into heaven. He loved all creatures and wouldn't hurt a fly; later in life he became a vegetarian. He died in Fort Wayne, Indiana. His obituary painted this portrait: "In the most inclement weather he might be seen barefooted and almost naked except when he chanced to pick up articles of old clothing. Notwithstanding the privations and exposure he endured, he lived to an extreme old age, 70 years . . . though no person would have judged from his appearance that he was 60." At the time of his death in 1847 he owned twelve hundred acres of land. As word about his apple planting work started to circulate, he soon became a folk hero. Today, many festivals throughout the Northeast and Midwest pay homage to Johnny Appleseed and his role in settling the frontier.

## APPLES IN MINNESOTA

When European settlers first came to Minnesota, they brought apples, planting varieties that hailed from Europe and had been cultivated in New England. Apples were

### A BUSHEL AND A PECK, A POUND OR A CUP; HOW DO APPLES MEASURE UP?

Buying and using apples can be confusing. How much is a bushel? How many pounds are needed for a pie? How many apples make a cup? Because apple sizes can vary from a little larger than a cherry to as big as a grapefruit, measurements are approximate. Pecks and bushels refer to the size of a bag or basket.

- A bushel is 42–48 pounds, about 126 apples
- A peck is 10–12 pounds, about 32 apples
- A half peck is 5–6 pounds, about 16 apples
- 2 pounds of apples are needed for a standard 9-inch pie
- A bushel of apples will yield about 20 quarts of applesauce
- About 36 apples will produce 1 gallon of apple cider
- A pound is 3–4 medium apples
- 1 large apple is usually about 2 cups chopped
- 1 medium apple is ¾ cup chopped

grown to eat fresh, to be cooked into all kinds of lovely dishes, and to be dried and preserved, but their primary use was for making hard cider, an essential component of frontier entertainment. There was one problem: the only apples that could survive the harsh Minnesota winters were crabapples.

In 1853 Peter Gideon moved to Minnesota and set up a homestead on Lake Minnetonka near Excelsior. He planted thousands of trees, but none of them survived more than a few years. Contemplating the only surviving tree, a Siberian crabapple, the determined horticulturist spent his last few dollars on a bushel of seeds from a grower in Bangor, Maine. As fate would have it, one of these seeds crossed with his Siberian crabapple to produce a cultivar that made it through Minnesota's harsh winters and yielded a wonderful-tasting apple that worked well for eating, cooking, and cider making. He named the apple Wealthy, after his wife, in 1868. Gideon generously shared his knowledge and

*Peter M Gideon.*

seedlings, the results of years of trial and error, with anyone who asked. It wasn't long before Wealthy apples were growing all over Minnesota. By the beginning of the 1900s the Wealthy was one of the top five apples grown nationally. It remains popular and was the parent for other successful apples, including the Haralson.

Gideon was an avid member of the Minnesota Horticultural Society. In 1879 the society lobbied the State of Minnesota to fund a test orchard for the development of apple breeds, and nearly thirty years later one was created near Victoria.

## A WORLD-RENOWNED APPLE-BREEDING PROGRAM

In a small, rural community about sixty minutes southwest of Minneapolis is one of only three apple breeding programs in the United States (the other two are at Washington State University and Cornell University). Since 1907, Chaska has been home to the University of Minnesota's Horticultural Research Center's apple-breeding program, which began in 1878. Despite Minnesota's rank of number twenty-seven for apple production in the United States, it is close to the top for apple breeding: to date, twenty-six different varieties have been released.

Initially the research center's main focus was to breed apples that were winter hardy and could survive at northern latitudes. Record-breaking cold in 1917–18 quickly helped define which apples could tolerate Minnesota's harsh winter weather. Today, quality, flavor, texture, and overall eating experience have become the driving forces behind the research, led by breeding program administrator Jim Luby.

What does it take to develop a world-

## A FRUITFUL LINEAGE: MINNESOTA'S APPLE "FAMILY TREE"

Twenty-seven astonishing apples have been released from the University of Minnesota apple breeding program. Here are the current favorites and some of the most notable:

1868   **Wealthy Peter Gideon** (pre-university cultivar)

1922   **Haralson; parents, Malinda x Wealthy**

1936   **Beacon; parent, Malinda** (open pollinated)

1940   **Prairie Spy; parents** undetermined

1943   **Fireside/Connell Red, the Minnesota Red Delicious; parents undetermined**

1946   **Chestnut Crabapple; parent, Malinda** (open pollinated)

1957   **Centennial Crabapple; parents, Dolgo x Wealthy**

1964   **Regent; parents, Red Duchess x Red Delicious**

1966   **Honeygold; parents, Golden Delicious x Haralson**

1970   **Red Baron; parents, Golden Delicious x Red Duchess**

1977   **State Fair; parents, Mantet x Oriole**

1977   **Sweet Sixteen; parents, Frostbite x Northern Spry**

1978   **Keepsake; parents, Frostbite x Northern Spry**

1991   **Honeycrisp; parents, Keepsake x unknown**   >>

| 1996 | Zestar!® (Minnewahta cultivar); parents, State Fair x MN 1691 |
| 2006 | SnowSweet® (Wildung cultivar); parents, Connell Red x Sharon |
| 2007 | SweeTango® (Minneiska cultivar); parents, Honeycrisp x Zestar! |
| 2008 | Frostbite™; parents undetermined |
| 2014 | MN55 (not yet named) |

In the early days of the breeding program, the emphasis was on producing cultivars that were winter hardy and disease resistant. Today, the emphasis is on flavor and texture. The following apples were important as methods and records were tested, but they are not produced today.

| 1920 | Minnehaha; Malinda (open pollinated) |
| 1922 | Wedge; Ben Davis (open pollinated) |
| 1922 | Folwell; Malinda (open pollinated) |
| 1942 | Minjon; unknown but possibly Jonathan x Wealthy |
| 1943 | Victory; McIntosh (open pollinated) |
| 1946 | Redwell; Scotts Winter (open pollinated) |
| 1949 | Oriole; parents undetermined |
| 1950 | Lakeland; Malinda (open pollinated) |
| 1957 | Northland Crab; McIntosh x Dolgo |

class apple? Time and testing and more testing. The research orchard has forty acres and twenty thousand trees. All of the breeding is through natural crossing, not genetic modification. Growers graft a potential seed onto dwarf rootstock and nurture a seedling in the greenhouse. As many as seven thousand seedlings get their start in the greenhouse, but only about 2,500 will leave it for the orchard. About three years after planting, the tree bears fruit. When the fruit is ready for harvest, it undergoes a battery of tests. David Bedford leads a team that tests five to six hundred apples per day throughout the harvest season. First and foremost is taste. About one percent of apples impress the team enough to continue to the next stage. The apples are assessed for visuals, aromas, and texture. They are measured for density, sugars, and acidity. Apple trees that fail are removed, and new specimens are planted the next year. The process is painstaking: it took twenty-nine years to develop the Honeycrisp and nineteen years to create the SweeTango.

## OUR HONEY, THE HONEYCRISP

Honeycrisp, the Minnesota state fruit, is loved around the world. Released from the University of Minnesota apple breeding program in 1991, this high-quality apple with exceptional taste and crunch has become the darling of the apple industry. The research team actually had to redefine its parameters for texture because of the Honeycrisp's explosive crispness. Before the Honeycrisp, apple texture was described as either soft or firm and measured scientifically in the lab. The density of firm or hard apples show in the range of 18 to 20 pounds of pressure. The Honeycrisp, at 14, is less dense but more juicy, characteristics that contribute to a crispness in each bite.

The first Minnesota apple to become a worldwide success, the Honeycrisp grows extremely well in areas with cool nights and moderate daytime temperatures—and for this reason the Upper Midwest produces the best. Its characteristic taste is a balance of sweet and tart with a great crunchy texture and ample juiciness. Beautiful to look at with its blushing bright red stripes over a yellowish green background, this apple is wonderful for eating fresh out of hand or using in salads because it is slow to oxidize and brown. In 2006, this incredible apple was honored as a significant technological discovery in *The Better World Report*. One more reason to love the Honeycrisp: it stores well for up to seven months. Look for it in orchards starting in late September.

# APPLE VARIETIES OF THE MIDWEST

| VARIETY | FLAVOR | TEXTURE | HARVESTTIME | USES | ORIGIN |
|---|---|---|---|---|---|
| Beacon | sweet/tart | soft | late August | fresh, sauce | Minnesota, 1936 |
| Chestnut Crab | sweet/nutty | chunky | early September | fresh, sauce | Minnesota, 1949 |
| Connell Red | sweet | crisp | late September | fresh, cooking, pie | *(see note)* |
| Cortland | sweet/tart | chunky | late September | fresh, salads, cooking | New York |
| Duchess (Past Prime) | tart | tender | early August | pie, sauce | New York |
| Fireside | sweet | firm | early October | fresh, salads, baking | Minnesota, 1943 |
| Frostbite™ | very sweet | firm | early October | cider | Minnesota, 2008 |
| Gala | sweet | firm | late August | fresh, cooking | *(see note)* |
| Ginger Gold | tangy | crisp | early September | fresh, cooking, pie | Virginia |
| Haralred | tart | crisp | late September | fresh, cooking, pie | *(see note)* |
| Haralson | tart | crisp | late September | fresh, cooking, pie | Minnesota, 1922 |
| Hazen | sweet | firm | late August | fresh, cooking | North Dakota, 1979 |
| Honeycrisp | sweet/tart | crisp | late September | fresh, salads | Minnesota, 1991 |
| Honeygold | sweet | firm | early October | fresh, cooking | Minnesota, 1970 |
| Keepsake | sweet/spicy | firm | early October | fresh, cooking | Minnesota, 1978 |
| Kinderkrisp | sweet/tart | crisp | early August | fresh, cooking | |
| La Crescent | sweet | crisp | early September | fresh, cooking | *(see note)* |
| Liberty | sweet/tart | firm | early October | fresh, cooking | New York |
| Lodi (yellow) | sweet | firm | mid-August | fresh, cooking | |
| Macoun | sweet/rich | firm | late September | fresh, cooking, pie, cider | New York |
| McIntosh | sweet | firm | mid-September | fresh, salads, cooking | |

| VARIETY | FLAVOR | TEXTURE | HARVESTTIME | USES | ORIGIN |
|---|---|---|---|---|---|
| Norland | tart | firm | late August | fresh, cooking | |
| Norwest Greening | sweet | soft | late September | cooking | |
| Paula Red | sweet | crisp | late August | fresh, pie, sauce | Michigan |
| Prairie Spy | sweet | firm | late October | baking | Minnesota, 1940 |
| Pristine | sweet | crisp | late August | fresh | |
| Red Baron | sweet | firm | mid-September | fresh | Minnesota, 1970 |
| Red Haralson | tart | crisp | mid-September | fresh, pie | *(see note)* |
| Redwell | sweet | firm | early October | fresh | |
| Regent | sweet/tart | firm | early October | fresh, cooking | Minnesota, 1964 |
| Sanza | sweet | firm | late August | baking | Japan |
| SnowSweet® | sweet/savory | crisp | early October | fresh | Minnesota, 2006 |
| State Fair | slightly tart | crisp | late August | fresh, cooking | Minnesota, 1977 |
| Sunrise | sweet | crisp | late August | fresh | Canada |
| Sweet Sixteen | very sweet | crisp | mid-late September | fresh, salads | Minnesota, 1977 |
| SweeTango® | sweet/spicy | crisp | early September | fresh, salads | Minnesota, 2009 |
| Vista Bella | sweet | firm | late August | fresh, cooking | |
| Wealthy | tart | tender | early September | fresh, pie, sauce | Minnesota, 1868 |
| Williams Pride | sweet/tart | crisp | late August | fresh | Illinois |
| Zestar!® | sweet/tart | tender | late August | fresh, cooking | Minnesota, 1999 |

*Notes:* The Connell Red, Haralred, and Red Haralson are the same apple with different names, a naturally occurring mutation of the Haralson. The Gala, hailing from New Zealand, is widely grown in Michigan and southern Wisconsin. The La Crescent apple, grown from a European cultivar at an orchard in La Crescent, Minnesota, is not widely available. You may encounter some of the less-well-known apples at an orchard or a grandparent's farm, but many of them are declining or not as tasty as the current superstars.

# BASICS

**H**arvesttime has arrived and you have your apple haul. What's next? Take full advantage of the variety and bounty and put up apples in numerous ways. Here are several basic recipes to fill your pantry with apple staples, components for a great many culinary excursions. Make up a batch of each and have them at the ready for whatever need may come your way. Ready, set, go!

## APPLE SPICE BLEND

*Many combinations fall into the category of "apple spice." Cinnamon, nutmeg, and cloves are classics for anything apple. If you happen to have all of the ingredients on hand, this recipe comes together quickly. It's easy to double if you think you will use it within three months. Don't stop at apple pie: this blend enhances many dishes, from oatmeal to pizza.* **MAKES ABOUT ⅓ CUP**

- ¼ cup plus 1 tablespoon ground cinnamon
- 1 teaspoon ground nutmeg
- 1 teaspoon ground cloves
- ½ teaspoon ground cardamom
- ½ teaspoon ground fenugreek, optional

Mix together all ingredients and store in a small glass jar. For best flavor, use within 3 months.

*Tip:* If you prefer to purchase a readymade blend, the Golden Fig in St. Paul, Minnesota, produces a lovely apple spice: goldenfig.com. ◊

## MULLING SPICE

*This simple blend of spices is a perfect accompaniment for Fresh Apple Cider (page 160). You can also mix it into hard cider or wine. Make a batch to give as gifts in little jars or cello bags.* **MAKES 4 HALF PINTS, ENOUGH FOR 8 GALLONS OF CIDER**

........................

1 orange (see tip)

1 cup sugar, plus more for rolling

12 cinnamon sticks

8 star anise

1 tablespoon freshly grated nutmeg

1 tablespoon whole cloves

1 tablespoon whole allspice berries

¼ cup coarsely chopped crystallized ginger

16 cardamom pods

........................

Cut the peel off the orange in 1-inch-wide strips. Be careful to cut just the outer peel and not the bitter white pith. Place 2 cups water in a small saucepan, set over medium-high heat, and bring to a low boil. Stir in the orange peels and simmer for 15 minutes. Drain and rinse peels; set aside.

Combine sugar with 1 cup water in a medium saucepan, set over medium-high heat, and bring to a boil. Add the orange peel. When the mixture returns to a boil, reduce heat and simmer for 30 minutes. Remove orange peels, roll in granulated sugar, and dry on a piece of parchment paper for up to 2 days. Reserve the syrup for another use. When the orange peel is dry, coarsely chop.

Crush the cinnamon sticks with a meat mallet. In a large bowl, stir together crushed cinnamon sticks, crystallized orange peel, star anise, grated nutmeg, cloves, allspice berries, ginger, and cardamom. Divide mixture into 4 wide-mouth, half-pint canning jars and seal. Use within 1 year: ¼ cup will spice half a gallon of cider.

*Tip:* Instead of making the fresh crystallized orange peel, substitute 1 tablespoon purchased orange peel. But fresh is better, and I highly recommend trying it at least once. ◇

## RAS EL HANOUT

*Many of the warm spices associated with apples are also found in Mediterranean cuisines. You may even already have the spices for this typical Moroccan combination on hand. If you prefer to buy a prepared blend, try McCormick brand.* **MAKES 2 TABLESPOONS**

    1 teaspoon cumin seeds
    2 coriander seeds
    6 allspice berries
    2 cardamom pods
    4 whole cloves
 1½ teaspoons cinnamon
  ½ teaspoon turmeric
  ¼ teaspoon mace
  ¼ teaspoon ground ginger
    1 teaspoon paprika
  ¼ teaspoon freshly grated nutmeg
    1 teaspoon freshly ground black pepper
  ½ teaspoon cayenne

In a small skillet set over medium heat, toast cumin, coriander, allspice, cardamom, and cloves until fragrant. Grind in a spice grinder. Mix with remaining spices. ◇

## Not-So-Old-Fashioned Applesauce

*Back in the day, making applesauce was a way to preserve autumn's bounty throughout the cold winter months. With a cache of applesauce in your larder, an abundant array of dishes are at your disposal. You may have an old recipe from your family's collection that calls for more sugar than this not-so-old-fashioned version does. Many of today's apples are sweeter than the heritage varieties available years ago. With that in mind, it's always best to taste the apples before adding sugar. You may be able to eliminate the sweetener altogether. This recipe can be doubled or quadrupled. Two of my favorite apples to make into sauce are Wealthy and Sweet Sixteen.* **MAKES 4 PINTS**

- 6 pounds apples, cored and cut into eighths
- ½ cup sugar (see tip)
- 1 tablespoon Apple Spice Blend (page 15), or substitute cinnamon (see tip)
- juice of 1 lemon
- 1 cup water

Mix apples with sugar, spice(s), lemon juice, and water in a heavy-bottomed pot. Cook the apple mixture over medium heat until bubbling and saucy, stirring occasionally, about 30 minutes. Add another cup of water if it becomes too thick and dry. Pass sauce through a food mill or sieve for a smooth texture and to remove the skin.

Sauce will keep in the refrigerator for about 7 days and in the freezer for 4 months. Canned sauce will keep in the pantry for 1 year, until the next apple season; refer to the Ball canning guide for specifics on canning procedures: www.freshpreserving.com.

*Tips:* Spoon fresh applesauce on top of hot oatmeal, granola, potato latkes, pancakes, or waffles or serve as a side with pork chops. Applesauce can be substituted for oil in many baked goods to make treats that are low in fat and sugar.

Instead of sugar, try honey, maple syrup, agave syrup, or stevia. Instead of cinnamon, try ginger, nutmeg, or cardamom. ◇

## SPICED APPLE BUTTER

*Here is a simple but nostalgic hostess or holiday gift. Cover the lid with brown parchment paper tied with natural cooking twine and tag for a rustic look. Add a nice loaf of artisanal seeded bread, and you have provided a memorable breakfast.* **MAKES 8 HALF PINTS**

3  pounds apples, peeled, cored, and chopped

½  cup Fresh Apple Cider (page 160)

1  teaspoon cinnamon

1  teaspoon minced fresh ginger

2  tablespoons honey

Place all ingredients in a heavy-bottomed saucepan. Cook over medium heat for about 40 minutes, stirring occasionally, until apples form a thick, spreadable sauce. Store in the refrigerator for up to 1 week, in the freezer for up to 4 months, or canned 1 year.

*Tip:* Refer to www.freshpreserving.com for safe canning procedures.  ◊

## GINGERY APPLE CHUTNEY

*This versatile savory sauce will become one of your pantry staples. Slather it on a sandwich, pair it with cheese, or spoon it onto a pork chop. A firm, tart apple works best for this recipe.* **MAKES 4 CUPS**

6 apples (Regent or Red Haralson; see head note), peeled, cored, and chopped

½ cup cider vinegar

1 cup packed light brown sugar

1 large sweet onion, chopped

2 tablespoons minced fresh ginger

1 teaspoon mustard seeds

1 teaspoon whole cloves

¼ teaspoon red pepper flakes, crushed

zest and juice of 1 lemon

1 cup golden raisins

In a large saucepan, combine the apples, cider vinegar, brown sugar, onions, ginger, mustard seeds, cloves, and red pepper flakes. Bring to a boil over medium-high heat. Reduce heat to medium and cook for about 45 minutes, stirring occasionally. Remove from heat and stir in lemon zest and juice and raisins. Allow mixture to cool, and then refrigerate. Chutney will keep for 2 weeks in the refrigerator, 2 months in the freezer, or 1 year canned.

*Tip:* Refer to www.freshpreserving.com for safe canning procedures. ◊

## APPLE GINGER CRANBERRY SAUCE

*This sauce is brilliant in color and flavor. The sweet apples tame the tart cranberries and in turn contrast with the peppery ginger and jalapeño. Choose a firm, tart apple like the Haralson. Serve with roasted turkey, salmon, or your favorite cheese.* **MAKES 4 PINTS**

1 (16-ounce) bag fresh cranberries

2 large apples (see head note), cored and chopped

¼ cup water

½ cup sugar

¼ cup chopped crystallized ginger

1 tablespoon minced fresh ginger

1 small jalapeño pepper, seeded and minced

pinch kosher salt

Combine cranberries, apples, water, and sugar in a medium saucepan. Cook over medium heat, stirring occasionally, until the cranberries burst and the apples begin to soften, about 10 minutes. Add the crystallized and fresh ginger and stir. Add the jalapeño and the salt. Continue to cook, stirring, for about 10 more minutes. Store in the refrigerator for up to 1 week, in the freezer for up to 4 months, or canned 1 year.

*Tip:* Refer to www.freshpreserving.com for safe canning procedures. ◇

## Apple Salsa

*This salsa offers another excellent way to combine the tart-sweet flavors of apples with the spicy, savory flavors of the Southwest. Serve with chips or nachos or use as a refreshing sauce for grilled or roasted chicken, halibut, or shrimp.* **MAKES 4 CUPS**

1 large firm, tart apple, cored and minced

2 tomatillos, husked and minced

½ cup minced red onion

1 red jalapeño, or substitute green, seeded and minced

1 clove garlic, minced

juice of 1 lime

½ teaspoon salt

½ cup chopped cilantro

2 tablespoons sunflower oil (Smude's) or canola oil

In a large bowl, mix together all ingredients. Cover and refrigerate for at least 30 minutes to allow flavors to mingle. The salsa will keep in the refrigerator for up to 4 days.  ◇

## DRIED APPLES

*Here is an easy way to enjoy the many varieties of apples well beyond harvest. Dried apples offer another layer of flavor and texture to create excitement in baked goods, hot cereal, and salads and also make a great addition to trail mixes or your snacking routine.* **MAKES 4 DOZEN SLICES**

4  cups water

juice of 1 lemon

6  medium apples

Preheat oven to 200 degrees. Line 2 large baking sheets with parchment paper and set aside. Combine the lemon juice and water in a medium bowl. Rinse the apples but do not peel or core. Using a sharp knife or mandoline, cut apples crosswise into thin, ⅛-inch slices and remove seeds. Soak slices in lemon water for 30 minutes. Drain slices and pat dry.

Arrange slices in a single layer on prepared baking sheets. Bake for 1 hour, then flip slices with a spatula. Bake for 1 more hour. For crispier apple slices, bake for an additional 30 to 60 minutes. Turn off the oven, crack open the door, and leave apples in the oven for another hour, until cool.

When cool, store in an airtight container. Apple slices will keep unrefrigerated for 1 week, refrigerated for 1 month, or in the freezer for 4 months.

*Tip:* For more information, see *The Beginner's Guide to Making and Using Dried Foods: Preserve Fresh Fruits, Vegetables, Herbs, and Meat with a Dehydrator, a Kitchen Oven, or the Sun* by Teresa Marrone. ◊

## CANDIED APPLE SLICES

*Candied apple slices are a lovely way to gild the lily. Use these jewels to gar-nish cakes, ice cream, and cocktails.* **MAKES 36–42 SLICES**

3 firm, tart apples

juice of 1 lemon

1 cup sugar

2 cups water

Rinse and dry apples. Place lemon juice in a bowl. Use a mandoline or sharp knife to slice the apples wafer thin; remove seeds. Dredge slices in the lemon juice to prevent apples from browning. In a heavy-bottomed saucepan set over medium-high heat, dissolve sugar in water and bring to a boil. Pour mixture into a glass bowl and plunge apple slices into the syrup. Cover bowl and let sit at room temperature for 8 hours or overnight.

Preheat oven to 225 degrees. Line a large baking sheet with parchment paper or silpat mat. Drain apple slices and carefully pat dry. Lay slices on prepared baking sheet. Bake for 30 minutes, then flip slices with a spatula. Bake for about 30 more minutes, until apples are dry. Cool com-pletely. Store in an airtight container for up to 2 weeks, or freeze for up to 3 months. ◊

# APPETIZERS

Apples' sweet nature lends itself so obviously to desserts, but you can also intrigue and tantalize by using this amazing fruit in savory and sweet appetizers. Pair refreshing apple flavors with herbs like rosemary and thyme or peppery spices like ginger and chiles.

## APPLE RUMAKI

*Rumaki, a longtime holiday party favorite, gets a remake with apples, cheese, and prosciutto, achieving the ever-popular salty and sweet flavor profile.* **MAKES 20 PIECES, TO SERVE 6**

......................

1 large firm, sweet-tart apple, peeled, cored, and cut into 20 wedges

10 thin slices prosciutto, sliced in half the long way

3 ounces fresh mozzarella, sliced into 20 slabs, or 20 mini balls

leaves from 2 sprigs rosemary, minced

freshly ground black pepper

......................

Preheat oven to 400 degrees. Line a baking sheet with parchment paper and set aside. Place an apple slice on one end of a prosciutto slice. Place a piece of cheese on top of the apple. Sprinkle with minced rosemary. Wrap the prosciutto around the apple and cheese, and lay bundle on prepared baking sheet. Repeat with remaining ingredients. Grind fresh pepper over the tops. Bake for about 12 minutes, until prosciutto is crispy and cheese is melted.

*Tip:* Switch up this appetizer with goat cheese and bacon. ◊

## APPLICIOUS BRUSCHETTA

*Bruschetta, pronounced* brewsketta, *is a favorite Italian appetizer of many variations, some served hot and some served cold. For a savory homegrown favorite, pair a Minnesota apple with a Minnesota blue cheese, award-winning products that will turn you into an award-winning host. Described as creamy and piquant, AmaBlu St. Pete's Select is produced by the Caves of Faribault in Faribault, Minnesota, and is named after the limestone caves it is aged in.* **MAKES 24 SLICES, TO SERVE 12**

- 1 tablespoon butter
- 1 tablespoon olive oil
- 1 red onion, sliced
- 2 tablespoons cider vinegar
- ¼ cup honey
- 2 large crisp, sweet-tart apples (SweeTango), cored and minced
- 2 tablespoons fresh thyme leaves
- 1 whole wheat baguette, sliced diagonally into 24 pieces
- ⅓ pound blue cheese (AmaBlu St. Pete's Select; see head note), crumbled

Preheat oven to 400 degrees. In a large skillet set over medium heat, melt the butter and add the olive oil. Add the onions and cook, stirring occasionally, until softened and caramelized, about 20 minutes. Add the cider vinegar and simmer for about 5 minutes. Stir in honey, apples, and thyme. Cook, stirring occasionally, until apples are softened and lightly browned.

Place the baguette slices on a rimmed baking sheet. Mound a spoonful of apple mixture on each slice. Top with about a tablespoon of crumbled blue cheese. Toast in the oven until the cheese is bubbly, about 10 minutes. Serve hot. ◊

## Apple–Pine Nut Tartlets

*These little jewels are so easy and so pretty. Choose a tart apple to counter the savory rich flavor of the chutney.* **MAKES 15, TO SERVE 5–7**

........................

1 tablespoon lemon juice

½ cup minced apple (see head note),
    plus 15 apple slivers for garnish

½ cup Gingery Apple Chutney (page 21)

1 tablespoon snipped fresh chives,
    plus 30 (1-inch) chive tips for garnish

½ cup mascarpone

2 tablespoons pine nuts, toasted

1 (1.9-ounce) package mini phyllo shells

........................

Prepare the apples. In a small bowl, combine lemon juice and 1 cup water. Toss minced apples in water and let sit for a few minutes, then drain. Combine the minced apple, chutney, snipped chives, mascarpone, and pine nuts, stirring to mix well. Spoon mixture into mini phyllo shells. Garnish with an apple sliver and 2 chive sprigs.  ◊

## Smoked Trout and Apple Tartlets

*I love the combination of chèvre, apples, and smoked trout. Fresh herbs along with goat cheese give this appetizer a French spin. Chervil is a little-used herb that has a delicate, fresh flavor. If you can't find chervil, substitute mint. Because there is no standard size for mini muffin tins, you will have to experiment to get the right size circle of dough. Somewhere between 3 and 4 inches should work.* **MAKES 24 APPETIZERS**

1  sheet refrigerated pie dough,
    or 1 single-crust pie dough round

4  ounces goat cheese

1  cup minced crisp, tart apple

1  cup shredded smoked trout

1  shallot, minced

zest and juice of 1 lemon

1  teaspoon minced fresh parsley

1  teaspoon minced fresh chervil (see head note)

1  teaspoon minced fresh tarragon

pinch salt

pinch black pepper

Preheat oven to 350 degrees. Use a small biscuit cutter to cut pie dough into 24 (3- to 4-inch) rounds (see head note). Press rounds into the cups of a mini muffin tin. Spoon a teaspoon of goat cheese into the bottom of each pie shell. In a medium bowl, lightly mix together the apple, trout, shallot, lemon zest and juice, parsley, chervil, tarragon, salt, and pepper. Spoon mixture into pie shells. Bake for about 25 minutes, until golden.  ◊

# Puff Pastry Apple Hors d'oeuvres

*Puff pastry dough takes common ingredients and elevates a recipe to fancy fare.* **MAKES 32, TO SERVE 10–15**

...........................

- 1 large red onion, sliced
- 1 apple, cored and chopped
- 1 tablespoon olive oil
- ¼ cup balsamic vinegar
- 1 tablespoon fresh rosemary
- ½ teaspoon sea salt
- ¼ teaspoon freshly ground black pepper
- 8 thin slices pancetta (3 ounces)
- 1 (17.3-ounce) package puff pastry dough, thawed
- 4 ounces Gruyère, shredded
- 2 tablespoons pine nuts

...........................

Preheat oven to 400 degrees. Line a rimmed baking sheet with parchment paper and set aside. In a large bowl, mix together the onion, apple, olive oil, balsamic vinegar, rosemary, salt, and pepper. Spread onion-apple mixture in a single layer on prepared baking sheet. Bake for 15 minutes. Stir and continue to bake for another 10 minutes. Lay the pancetta slices on another baking sheet and roast for about 10 minutes, until crispy. When cool enough to handle, coarsely chop the pancetta.

Unfold the dough on a work surface and flatten lightly with a rolling pin. Cut each sheet 4 times crosswise and 4 times lengthwise to make 16 squares. Line 2 baking sheets with parchment paper and transfer dough to sheets. Poke the middle of each square with a fork. Top each square with an equal amount of onion-apple topping. Sprinkle with the Gruyère, pancetta, and pine nuts. Bake for about 15 minutes, until pastry is golden and cheese is bubbling. Serve hot. ◊

## APPLE-FILLED PHYLLO PURSES

*The whimsical phyllo purse is light and flaky, a delicate little pouch holding a luscious surprise.* **MAKES 12 APPETIZERS**

- 1 tablespoon olive oil
- 1 apple, cored and chopped
- 1 cup minced sweet onion
- 4 strips applewood-smoked bacon, chopped
- 1 tablespoon minced fresh ginger
- ½ cup Fresh Apple Cider (page 160)
- 1 tablespoon fresh thyme leaves
- 1 (16-ounce) package phyllo dough, thawed
- 8 tablespoons (1 stick) butter, melted
- 1 cup shredded Gouda with fenugreek (Marieke) or substitute plain Gouda
- 12 chives

Preheat oven to 350 degrees. In a skillet set over medium-high heat, warm the olive oil and then add apples, onions, and bacon. Cook, stirring, until the apples and onions are soft and the bacon is browned. Stir in ginger, cider, and thyme and continue to cook until liquid is absorbed. Set aside.

Grease a 12-cup muffin tin. Remove phyllo dough from package. Lay 1 sheet on a work surface and cover remaining with a tea towel. Working quickly, lightly brush sheet with butter. Lay another sheet on top and brush with butter. Repeat with 2 more sheets. Cut the dough into 6-inch squares. Press dough into the muffin cups. Spoon ⅓ cup of apple filling into each phyllo shell and top with Gouda. Repeat the process with another 4 sheets of dough and filling and cheese. Gather up the edges of the pastry and twist shut. Tie with a piece of chive. Bake for 30 minutes, until golden brown. ◇

# Ancient Grains and Apple Cakes

*Many cakes fit the appetizer category: crab cakes, blini, and crêpes, to name a few. This rendition uses ancient grains, capitalizing on their earthy flavors and chewy texture. Add a salad to this starter and you have a scrumptious light lunch.* **MAKES 12 APPETIZERS, TO SERVE 6**

........................

### SAUCE

- 1 tablespoon canola or sunflower oil
- 1 apple, cored and chopped
- 1 cup chopped sweet onion
- ½ cup apple cider
- 1 tablespoon chopped fresh rosemary
- ½ teaspoon salt
- ¼ teaspoon freshly ground black pepper

### CAKES

- ⅓ cup wild rice
- 4 cups chicken stock
- ⅓ cup green wheat freekeh (see tip)
- ⅓ cup quinoa
- ½ cup canola or sunflower oil, divided
- 2 cups minced apples
- 1 cup minced onions
- 2 cloves garlic, minced
- 4 large eggs, lightly beaten
- 1 teaspoon Ras el Hanout (page 17; see tip)
- ½ teaspoon salt
- ¼ teaspoon freshly ground black pepper
- 1 cup plain Greek-style yogurt

........................

Place all sauce ingredients in a large skillet set over medium-high heat. Cook, stirring, until the apples and onions are soft and the cider is absorbed, then remove from heat and set aside. The sauce can be made ahead of time.

In a large saucepan set over medium-high heat, combine wild rice and stock and bring to a boil. Reduce heat, cover, and simmer for 15 minutes. Stir in the green wheat freekeh and continue to simmer for another 15 minutes. Stir in the quinoa and simmer for another 15 minutes or until grains are tender. Remove from heat and let cool; drain any excess stock.

In a skillet set over medium heat, warm ¼ cup oil and add the 2 cups apples, 1 cup onions, and garlic. Cook, stirring, until soft and translucent. Remove from heat. In a large bowl, mix together the grains, cooked apple mixture, eggs, and seasonings. Let sit for a few minutes to allow flavors to blend. Use your hands to form mixture into 12 small cakes, about 3 inches in diameter.

In a large skillet, heat the remaining ¼ cup oil over medium-high heat. When it begins to shimmer, add the cakes, being careful not to overcrowd the pan. Fry for about 4 minutes, until golden brown, and then carefully turn over. After another 4 to 5 minutes, when golden brown and crispy, remove cakes from oil and drain on paper towels. Repeat with remaining cakes.

Arrange 2 cakes per plate and serve with a spoonful of the sauce and a dollop of plain Greek yogurt.

*Tips:* Green wheat freekeh refers to an ancient wheat that is toasted and cracked. The flavor is nutty and the texture is chewy. Boasting a high protein content, it has a lower glycemic index than brown rice. Substitute brown rice, barley, farro, or spelt.

Instead of Ras el Hanout, use Apple Spice Blend (page 15) and add ¼ teaspoon cayenne.  ◊

## Gorgonzola Apple Pizzetti

*This little appetizer is an elegant rendition of the flat, cracker-bread pizzas that are a mainstay of gastropub fare. I prefer a crisp, tart apple, but many different types can be used. If you choose one that browns easily, bathe slices in lemon water until you are ready to assemble the dish. This recipe is easy to double or triple.* **SERVES 2**

2 (8x4-inch) artisanal crackers (La Panzanella)

1 apple, peeled, cored, and sliced thin (see head note)

2 ounces Gorgonzola dolce

1 tablespoon honey

1 tablespoon pine nuts

Preheat oven to 400 degrees. Lay the crackers on a baking sheet. Cover the crackers with a layer of apples. Sprinkle Gorgonzola on top, and drizzle honey and pine nuts on top of the cheese. Bake for about 8 minutes, until the cheese is bubbling. ◊

## NOT LIKE ANY OTHER NACHOS

*My husband's favorite guilty pleasure is nachos. Here is a way to bump up the nutrition so you can enjoy with less guilt.* **SERVES 4**

............................

- 6 cups tortilla chips
- 1 (5-ounce) package power greens blend (kale, chard, spinach), rinsed and spun dry
- 2 cups chopped rotisserie chicken
- 1 cup cooked or canned chickpeas
- 1 cup shredded Cheddar (Widmer's)
- 2 apples, cored and chopped
- 1 bunch green onions, sliced
- ¼ cup pepitas (pumpkin seeds) or sunflower seeds
- 1 cup Greek-style yogurt
- 1 chipotle pepper in adobo sauce, minced
- 1 bunch cilantro, chopped (1 cup)
- 1 cup Apple Salsa (page 23)

............................

Preheat oven to 400 degrees. Spread the tortilla chips onto a large oven-proof platter. Layer the greens on top of the chips. Next, scatter the chicken, chickpeas, cheese, apples, onions, and pepitas over the greens. Bake until the cheese is melted, about 10 minutes.

Meanwhile, in a small bowl, mix together the yogurt and minced chipotle. Garnish heated nachos with cilantro. Spoon the chipotle yogurt onto one end of the platter and place the salsa in a small bowl on the other end. Enjoy! ◊

## MOODY BLUE BITES

*One of the first appetizers Rosebud Grocery was famous for were grapes that were hand rolled in a Gorgonzola cheese mixture and then in pistachios. I love this apple-y riff made with Moody Blue cheese, a natural smoked blue cheese from Roth cheese company in Wisconsin. Pump up the smoky flavor with chopped smoked almond.* **MAKES 36 BITES**

⅓ pound blue cheese (Roth Moody Blue; see head note)

4 ounces cream cheese

1 clove garlic, minced

pinch salt

2 medium crisp, tart apples, cored and minced

1 cup smoked almonds, chopped

Mix together the blue cheese, cream cheese, garlic, salt, and apples. Place chopped almonds in a small, flat dish. Take a spoonful of the cheese mixture and roll into a ball the size of a large marble. Roll cheese ball in chopped nuts. Repeat with remaining ingredients. ◇

## BRIE WITH APPLE CHUTNEY

*Brie and apples are a natural combination, so common as to run the risk of seeming passé. To make this cheese course stellar instead of ho-hum, choose a really good Brie to pair with a lovely homemade apple chutney. My favorite Brie is made in Mankato, Minnesota, at Alemar Cheese. This cheese is luscious and buttery. Add a few fresh apples that are juicy and crisp, and your taste buds will be dancing.* **SERVES 8–10**

16 ounces large unsalted cashews

 1 tablespoon unsalted butter, melted

 1 tablespoon honey

 2 tablespoons minced fresh thyme

½ teaspoon cayenne

½ teaspoon smoked paprika

 1 teaspoon sea salt

12 ounces Brie (Alemar Blue Earth; see head note)

½ cup Gingery Apple Chutney (page 21)

 2 apples, cored and sliced thin

 1 baguette, sliced

Preheat oven to 350 degrees. Spread cashews onto a rimmed baking sheet and toast in the oven for about 6 minutes. In a medium bowl, stir together the melted butter with honey, thyme, cayenne, paprika, and salt. Toss cashews in butter-spices mixture and spread on a piece of parchment paper to cool. Coarsely chop ¼ cup cashews to garnish the Brie.

Place the Brie in the center of a cheese platter. Slather with the apple chutney. Sprinkle the chopped cashews on top. Arrange apple slices and baguette slices around the Brie and add reserved chopped cashews.  ◈

## Fresh Ricotta with Apple Slices

*Here is a wonderful and versatile way to enjoy an assortment of apples from an orchard visit. Traditional ricotta is made with the leftover whey from the cheese-making process, so technically this isn't a true ricotta. Still, I call it DIY delicious!* **SERVES 8–10**

........................

|       |                                          |
|-------|------------------------------------------|
| 8     | cups whole milk (organic preferred)      |
| 1     | cup heavy cream (organic preferred)      |
| 3     | tablespoons white vinegar                |
| ½     | teaspoon salt                            |
| 3     | tablespoons honey                        |
| 2     | tablespoons chopped walnuts, toasted     |
| 3–4   | apples, cored and sliced thin            |

........................

In a medium heavy-bottomed saucepan set over medium heat, mix together the milk and cream and bring to a simmer. As soon as the milk starts to become foamy, check the temperature: it should be about 170 degrees. Continue to simmer for about 15 minutes, but do not let mixture boil or go over 185 degrees. Remove from heat. Add the vinegar and stir. Add the salt and stir. Cover the pot and let stand at room temperature for 2 hours to allow curds to form.

Set a large colander lined with cheesecloth over a large bowl. Spoon the curds into the cheesecloth. Gather up the corners and twist to squeeze out the excess whey (see tip). Let the ricotta sit for 30 minutes. Then gently squeeze out the excess moisture.

Mound the ricotta in the center of a large platter. Drizzle with honey and sprinkle with nuts. Arrange the apple slices around the edge and let everyone dip away.

*Tip:* Save the nutritious whey for another use, such as in a morning apple smoothie. ◇

# BREAKFAST, BRUNCH, and BREADS

pples lend themselves wonderfully to any brunch or breakfast. Little apple gems find their way into many classic recipes: from muffins and scones to luscious custardy egg bakes, they make everything better. At the day's most important meal, apples of any variety are worth savoring.

## THE NEW PORRIDGE

*Many different grains and rices are delicious as hot breakfast cereals. If you are using barley or quinoa for a dinner side, soup, or stew, make extra for a nutritious morning boost. That's called a planned-over, not a leftover.*

**SERVES 4**

*Choose a grain*

1 cup quinoa with 1 cup water; simmer 15 minutes

1 cup steel-cut oatmeal with 4 cups water; simmer 30 minutes

1 cup barley with 3 cups water; simmer 45 minutes

1 cup almond or regular milk

1 apple, cored and chopped

1 cup Not-So-Old-Fashioned Applesauce (page 18)

1 tablespoon ground flaxseed

¼ cup honey

1 tablespoon Apple Spice Blend (page 15)

¼ cup chopped almonds, walnuts, or pecans

¼ cup chia seeds

1 cup Greek-style yogurt

Divide cooked grains among 4 bowls, and then divide remaining ingredients among the bowls.

*Tips:* The grains can be made ahead of time and also used in combination. I like to portion out the ingredients, in the order listed, into a wide-mouth pint jar for on-the-go breakfasts. The jars will keep in the refrigerator for up to 4 days. Heat in the microwave when you're ready to eat. For a brunch side dish, divide into wide-mouth half-pint jars.  ◊

## SOUTHWESTERN APPLE OMELET

*Here is my take on the Denver omelet. As more varieties of fresh chiles become available, it's fun to take a classic to a new level. The poblano is a beautiful dark green with a complex, flavorful flesh. The seeds can have quite a bit of heat, so be careful when handling them: use gloves and wash your hands well.* **SERVES 2**

1 tablespoon olive oil

2 slices applewood-smoked bacon, chopped

½ cup chopped onion

½ cup sliced mushrooms

1 apple, cored and chopped, plus slices for serving

½ poblano chile, seeds and veins removed, chopped

4 large eggs

1 tablespoon water

pinch kosher salt

freshly ground black pepper

½ cup shredded extra-sharp Cheddar

Heat a medium skillet over medium-high heat. Add the olive oil and then the bacon. Add the onions and cook, stirring occasionally, for about 5 minutes, until the onions begin to turn golden brown. Stir in the mushrooms and cook for an additional 4 to 5 minutes. Stir in the apple and poblano and cook until soft. In a small bowl, whisk together eggs, water, salt, and a twist of pepper. Pour mixture into the skillet and cover. Let the eggs set for a few minutes, and then lift up the edges with a spatula on each of the 4 sides to let the uncooked egg seep underneath. Replace cover. When the omelet looks just about done, sprinkle with cheese, cover, and cook for about 2 more minutes. When the cheese is melted, fold the omelet in half. To serve, cut in half and place on 2 plates. Garnish with sliced apples. ◇

# HONEY APPLE CHALLAH EGG BAKE

*The combination of rich, eggy challah bread with apples and honey reminds me of Rosh Hashanah, the Jewish New Year, which is celebrated in the fall. Eating symbolic foods such as apples dipped in honey invokes a sweet new year. If you can't find challah, substitute a brioche or cinnamon bread.*

**SERVES 12**

1 loaf challah, cubed

8 large eggs

2 cups (1 pint) heavy cream

½ cup sugar

2 teaspoons vanilla

1 tablespoon Apple Spice Blend (page 15)

2 apples, cored and chopped

½ cup chopped pecans

8 tablespoons (1 stick) butter, cut into half-inch cubes

⅓ cup honey

Preheat oven to 375 degrees. Place challah in a large bowl and set aside. In a medium bowl, mix together the eggs, cream, sugar, vanilla, and spice blend. Pour onto the bread cubes and mix. Add the apples and pecans and mix well to distribute evenly. Grease a 9x13–inch ovenproof dish with some of the butter. Pour the bread mixture into the baking dish and dot with the remaining pieces of butter. Drizzle with honey. Let everything soak together for about 30 minutes. Bake for about 45 minutes, until top is golden brown and center is firm. If the top is browning too quickly, cover with aluminum foil. ◊

# DUTCH BABY

*Many cultures make a pancake that puffs up in the oven. The style I love is called Dutch baby, and this version is triply apple-y, with apple cider and apples in the topping and more apples in the eggy pancake. Any fresh-from-the-orchard apples can be used for this fun and delicious breakfast. You can make the topping ahead of time and then heat through for serving.* **SERVES 4**

**TOPPING**

- 2 tablespoons butter
- 1 apple, cored and minced
- 2 cups Fresh Apple Cider (page 160)
- 1 teaspoon Apple Spice Blend (page 15)
- ¼ cup honey

**PANCAKE**

- 4 tablespoons (½ stick) butter, divided
- 2 apples, cored and chopped
- 2 tablespoons honey
- 4 large eggs
- ¾ cup whole milk
- 1 cup white whole wheat flour
- 1 teaspoon vanilla
- 1 teaspoon Apple Spice Blend (page 15)
- ¼ teaspoon sea salt
- ¼ cup sliced almonds

In a saucepan set over medium heat, combine topping ingredients, stir, and bring to a simmer. Cook, stirring occasionally, until mixture is reduced and thick, about 25 minutes. Set aside and keep warm.

Preheat oven to 425 degrees. Set a medium skillet over medium heat and add 2 tablespoons butter. When butter sizzles, add the apples and honey. Cook, stirring, until softened, about 5 minutes.

Set a medium cast-iron pan over high heat. In a medium bowl, whisk together eggs, milk, flour, vanilla, spice blend, and salt. When the pan is hot, add the remaining 2 tablespoons butter, swirl, and then pour in the honey apples and the batter. Bake in the oven for about 15 minutes, until golden brown. Divide onto 4 plates and serve with warm apple topping and a sprinkle of almonds. ◊

## BRUNCHIE APPLE BREAD PUDDING

*Savory bread pudding is easy to put together and can be baked ahead of time and then rewarmed when you are ready to serve. Choose a baking apple that will retain a chunkier texture: McIntosh, Cortland, Haralson, or Regent.*

**SERVES 12**

12 ounces applewood-smoked bacon

8 tablespoons (1 stick) butter, divided

1 loaf artisanal whole-grain bread, cubed (10 cups)

3 apples, cored and chopped

1 onion, chopped

½ cup hard or regular apple cider

2 cups (1 pint) heavy cream

4 large eggs, beaten

8 ounces Emmenthaler, shredded

4 ounces Gruyère, shredded

1 tablespoon minced fresh thyme

½ teaspoon salt

½ teaspoon freshly ground black pepper

Preheat oven to 375 degrees. Line a rimmed baking sheet with aluminum foil and arrange bacon slices on it. Roast for 20 minutes. Drain slices on paper towels. When cool enough to handle, chop bacon and set aside.

Melt 4 tablespoons butter. In a large bowl, toss bread with melted butter, then set aside. In a large skillet set over medium-high heat, melt 2 tablespoons butter. Add the apples and onions and cook, stirring occasionally, until translucent, about 10 minutes. Add the cider, stir, and remove from heat. In a medium bowl, mix together heavy cream and eggs. Stir

in the cheeses, thyme, salt, and pepper. Pour the apple mixture and the egg mixture over the bread cubes and stir with a large spatula to combine. Let sit for at least 30 minutes so the bread can absorb the liquid.

Grease a 9x13–inch ovenproof dish or a jumbo muffin tin with remaining 2 tablespoons butter. Pour the bread into the baking dish or divide equally among muffin cups. Sprinkle with chopped bacon. Bake until golden, about 40 minutes for the baking dish and 30 minutes for the jumbo muffins. ◊

## ORCHARD BREAKFAST TART

*While we typically think of eggs for breakfast, this lovely tart could be served for brunch or lunch or a light dinner. Choose a firm, sweet-tart apple.*

**SERVES 6**

.............................

**SHELL**

1¼ cups unbleached all-purpose flour

½ teaspoon fine sea salt

8 tablespoons (1 stick) cold unsalted butter, cut into half-inch cubes

3–4 tablespoons ice water

**FILLING**

2 tablespoons unsalted butter

1 apple, cored and chopped

1 leek, rinsed and sliced

¼ cup apple brandy

8 large eggs, lightly beaten

½ cup crème fraîche, or substitute sour cream plus 1 tablespoon honey

¼ teaspoon salt

¼ teaspoon freshly ground black pepper

⅛ teaspoon cayenne

4 ounces mushroom Brie (Champion; see tip), chopped

.............................

For the tart dough, in a medium bowl, mix together the flour and salt. Use a pastry blender or two forks to mix the 8 tablespoons butter into the flour. Gradually drip in the cold water and blend in until the dough starts to come together. Turn onto a floured work surface and knead for a few minutes. Form a round flattened disk, wrap in plastic, and chill in the refrigerator for at least 1 hour.

Unwrap chilled dough and place on a floured work surface. Rap a few times with a rolling pin. Roll the dough into a 12-inch circle. Place into a 10-inch tart pan with a removable bottom, pressing dough up the sides and trimming excess off the top. Prick the bottom with a fork. Line the dough-filled pan with a sheet of parchment paper and fill with pie weights or dried beans. Chill in the freezer for at least 30 minutes. When ready to bake, put the tart shell directly from the freezer into a 425-degree oven. Bake for 8 to 10 minutes, then remove pie weights and set shell aside.

To prepare the filling, melt the 2 tablespoons butter in a large skillet set over medium-high heat. Add the apples and leeks and cook, stirring occasionally, for about 5 minutes, until tender. Pour in the apple brandy and cook to reduce the liquid, scraping the bottom of the pan to loosen any browned bits. Spoon mixture into the baked tart shell. In a medium bowl, mix together the eggs, crème fraîche, salt, pepper, and cayenne. Pour egg mixture over the apples and leeks, and sprinkle the Brie on top. Bake for about 25 minutes, until the top is golden brown and the center is set. Remove from oven and let sit for a few minutes before slicing.

*Tip:* If you can't find Champion, use a good-quality Brie and add 1 cup fresh sliced mushrooms to the skillet with the apples and leeks. ✧

## APPLE AND BACON–STUFFED FRENCH TOAST

*This recipe was inspired by my friend Kari Skibbie at Holland American Cheese, makers of Marieke Gouda. I loved her decadent french toast, but it was missing apples. I guarantee that this is more than a little over the top.*

**SERVES 4**

. . . . . . . . . . . . . . . . . . . . . . . . . .

### TOPPING

    1   apple, cored and minced

    2   cups Fresh Apple Cider (page 160)

    1   teaspoon Apple Spice Blend (page 15)

    ¼   cup honey


### TOAST

    1½   cups half-and-half, warmed

    2    large eggs

    2    tablespoons brown sugar

    ¾    teaspoon cinnamon

    2    tablespoons butter, melted, plus 2–3 tablespoons, softened

    2    teaspoons vanilla

    8    slices hearty white bread

    1    large apple, peeled, cored, and sliced

    1    pound cooked bacon

    6    ounces Gouda with fenugreek (Marieke) or plain Gouda, shredded

. . . . . . . . . . . . . . . . . . . . . . . . . .

In a large saucepan set over medium-high heat, stir together the topping ingredients and bring to a simmer. Cook for about 20 minutes, until mixture thickens. Set aside.

In a medium bowl, whisk together the half-and-half, eggs, brown sugar, cinnamon, melted butter, and vanilla. Transfer mixture to a large shallow dish.

Set a large skillet over medium heat and coat with cooking spray. Soak 1 slice of bread in egg mixture for about 1 minute and then add to skillet. Cook 4 to 5 minutes, until golden brown, then flip and continue to cook until both sides are golden brown. Repeat with remaining bread.

On a clean work surface, lay out French toast. Divide apple slices and bacon among 4 slices of bread and top each with one-quarter of the cheese. Top each with a remaining slice of toast and press down gently to set. Spread the sandwich tops with half of the softened butter.

Set a griddle over medium-high heat. Place the sandwiches buttered-side down on the hot griddle. Spread the remaining side of each sandwich with the remaining butter. Cook until crispy and golden brown and cheese is starting to melt, then flip and continue cooking until cheese is completely melted, about 3 minutes per side. Serve immediately with apple syrup topping. ◇

## APPLE NUT BREAD

*This bread freezes well and can be made into six to eight smaller loaves (see tip). Stock up and you will always have a snack or dessert at the ready.*

**MAKES 2 (8x4–INCH) LOAVES**

- 2 apples, cored and chopped
- 2½ cups unbleached all-purpose flour
- ½ cup whole wheat flour
- 1 teaspoon baking soda
- 1 teaspoon salt
- 1 cup chopped walnuts
- 2 large eggs
- 1 cup packed brown sugar
- ½ cup honey
- 1 cup Not-So-Old-Fashioned Applesauce (page 18)
- ¼ cup chia seeds
- 2 tablespoons Apple Spice Blend (page 15)
- ½ cup old-fashioned oats, divided

Preheat oven to 325 degrees. Grease 2 (8x4–inch) loaf pans and set aside. In a large bowl, mix together apples, flours, baking soda, salt, and walnuts. Use a mixer to beat the eggs with the brown sugar and honey. Add the applesauce, chia seeds, and spice blend. Pour into apple mixture and stir to combine. Sprinkle half of the oats on the bottoms of the prepared pans. Divide the dough between the 2 pans, and sprinkle with remaining oats. Bake for about 1 hour and 25 minutes, until a wooden pick inserted in the center comes out clean. Let cool in pan for 10 minutes, then remove and cool on rack.

*Tips:* For mini loaves, fill 3x5-inch pans three-quarters full and bake as directed. Begin checking for doneness after 45 to 50 minutes. To freeze, cool completely and then store individually in freezer bags. ◇

## APPLE HONEY MUFFINS

*Yes, there is such a thing as white whole wheat flour. This naturally developed wheat is lighter in flavor and color than regular whole wheat flour but has all of the same benefits. It's a great option for baked goods that pack a nutritional punch with a light texture. Freeze these muffins to have available for quick breakfasts on the go. Any baking apple will work here.* **MAKES 12 MUFFINS**

1½  cups white whole wheat flour

¼  cup ground flaxseed

1½  teaspoons baking powder

¼  teaspoon baking soda

2  teaspoons Apple Spice Blend (page 15; see tip)

¼  teaspoon salt

¾  cup packed brown sugar, divided

8  tablespoons (1 stick) butter, softened, plus 3 tablespoons, softened

¼  cup honey

2  large eggs

½  cup almond or regular milk

½  cup Greek-style yogurt

2  apples, cored and minced

½  cup sliced almonds

¼  cup old-fashioned oatmeal

½  teaspoon cinnamon

Preheat oven to 350 degrees. Line a muffin tin with papers and set aside. In a large bowl, whisk together the flour, flaxseed, baking powder, baking soda, spice blend, and salt. Set aside. Use a mixer to combine ½ cup brown sugar and 8 tablespoons butter, mixing on medium speed. Add the honey and eggs, one at a time, and mix for 2 minutes, until fluffy. Mix in the almond milk and yogurt. With mixer on low speed, blend in the dry ingredients just until combined. Reserve 2 tablespoons apples and 2 tablespoons almonds for topping. Fold in remaining apples and almonds by hand. Scoop muffin batter into tins, filling three-quarters full.

In a medium bowl, mix together reserved apples and almonds, oatmeal, remaining ¼ cup brown sugar, cinnamon, and remaining 3 tablespoons butter using a pastry blender or two forks. Sprinkle topping evenly over muffins. Bake for about 18 minutes, until golden brown and a wooden pick inserted in the center comes out clean.

*Tip:* If you don't have Apple Spice Blend, substitute 1 teaspoon cinnamon, ½ teaspoon nutmeg, ¼ teaspoon cardamom, and ¼ teaspoon ground cloves. ◊

## APPLE-STUDDED SCONES

*My mum, Evelyn, who was born and raised in Calgary, passed along the recipe for a special treat: tender, moist, and rich scones (pronounced* skahnz, *to rhyme with* fawns). *At the Rosebud Grocery, they were a weekly offering, and we made several varieties, with currants (traditional) or golden raisins or blueberries or, in autumn—my favorite—apples. Hot out of the oven, they are heavenly. Split them in half and spread with apple butter.* **MAKES 24 SCONES**

3½ cups unbleached all-purpose flour

½ cup cornstarch

½ cup granulated sugar

½ teaspoon salt

1 tablespoon plus 2 teaspoons baking powder

1 cup (2 sticks) cold unsalted butter, cut into half-inch cubes

1¼ cups buttermilk

4 large eggs

2 cups chopped apple (Haralson or Honeycrisp)

1 tablespoon raw or turbinado sugar

½ teaspoon cinnamon

Preheat oven to 425 degrees. Line 2 baking sheets with parchment paper and set aside. In a large bowl, whisk together the dry ingredients (flour through baking powder). Using a pastry cutter or two forks, blend in the butter until it is the size of peas. In a large measuring cup, beat the buttermilk and eggs. Reserve 1 tablespoon of the egg mixture to brush the tops of the scones. Pour remaining egg mixture into flour mixture and mix with a wooden spoon, being careful not to overmix. Dough will be lumpy. Fold in the apples, stirring gently to combine. Turn the dough out of the bowl onto a floured work surface. Pat lightly into a 12x9–inch rectangle, then cut into 12 (3x3–inch) squares. Cut each square in half diagonally. Brush the tops with the reserved egg mixture.

In a small bowl, stir together raw sugar and cinnamon. Sprinkle mixture on top of scones. Transfer scones to the prepared baking sheets. Bake for about 20 minutes, until golden.  ◊

## Cheddar Apple Cornbread

*This side dish is nice with chili after you've visited the orchard and want apples in everything. We love it with our Thanksgiving dinner, too. Cheddar and apples are a classic combination, kicked up a notch here with jalapeño peppers.* **SERVES 12**

3 cups unbleached all-purpose flour

1 cup yellow cornmeal

2 tablespoons baking powder

2 teaspoons kosher salt

1½ cups milk

4 large eggs, lightly beaten

9 tablespoons (1 stick plus 1 tablespoon) unsalted butter, melted

¼ cup honey

½ cup sunflower or canola oil

1 large apple (State Fair or SweeTango), cored and chopped

8 ounces sharp Cheddar, shredded

2 tablespoons seeded and minced jalapeño pepper

Preheat oven to 350 degrees. Grease a 9x13–inch baking dish. In a large bowl, stir together the flour, cornmeal, baking powder, and salt. In a separate bowl, mix together the milk, eggs, butter, honey, and sunflower oil. Stir the wet ingredients into the dry ingredients, being careful not to overmix. Stir in the apples, Cheddar, and jalapeño. Pour batter into the prepared pan. Bake for 30 to 35 minutes, until golden and a wooden pick inserted in the center comes out clean. Cool and cut into squares. ◊

# SALADS

Apples are a perfect counterpoint to the many savory elements found in salads. A nutritionally dense superfood, they provide sweetness, tartness, crunch, and lovely visual appeal. Leave the peel on for the greatest health benefit, not to mention the beautiful color. If you choose an apple that browns quickly, give your slices a quick rinse in a bowl of cold water mixed with the juice of one lemon before tossing with the rest of the salad. Most of these recipes call for one or two apples. If your apple is large, about the size of a baseball, it will yield about 2 cups. Plan for about ½ cup to 1 cup of apple per serving. And don't worry too much about exact measurements; if you have extra apple, just toss it in. It certainly won't hurt.

## APPLEPANZANELLA

*Inspired by the Italian bread salad* panzanella, *this recipe calls for roasting apples, onion, and Brussels sprouts to bring out their rich, deep, sweet flavors. I recommend the crisp SweeTango for this preparation. If you try another type of apple, make sure it has a firm texture that will not cook down or lose its shape when roasting.* SERVES 8

2  large apples (see head note), cored and chopped

1  cup chopped red onion

1  pound Brussels sprouts, trimmed and halved

4  cups cubed ciabatta

6  tablespoons extra-virgin olive oil, divided

sea salt and freshly ground black pepper

1  cup chopped walnuts

¼ cup cider vinegar

1 tablespoon honey

1 clove garlic, minced

¾ cup chopped Italian parsley

4 ounces Gouda (Marieke), shredded

..........................

Preheat oven to 400 degrees. In a large bowl, combine apples, onions, Brussels sprouts, and ciabatta. Toss with 2 tablespoons olive oil and sprinkle with salt and pepper. Spread mixture onto a rimmed baking sheet and roast for about 20 minutes, until soft and golden. Spread walnuts onto another small baking pan and roast for about 10 minutes. Let both pans cool.

In a small bowl, whisk together the cider vinegar, honey, and garlic and add a pinch of salt and pepper. Slowly add the remaining 4 tablespoons olive oil, whisking to blend. In a large bowl, toss the roasted apples, vegetables, and walnuts. Add the vinaigrette and toss to coat. Add parsley and cheese, tossing to combine. Taste and add salt and pepper if desired. ◊

## A to Z Spirals

*Perfect for a dinner party on the deck with friends, this salad is wonderful for early August, when the season's first apples are being harvested and zucchini is plentiful in the garden. If you don't have a "spiralizer," use a vegetable peeler to make thin planks and then cut those into thin strips.* **SERVES 4**

¼ cup chopped walnuts

4 cups torn butter lettuce, rinsed and spun dry

1 medium fennel bulb, sliced thin

½ medium red onion, sliced thin

1 medium tart apple, spiralized (see head note)

juice of 1 lemon

1 medium zucchini, spiralized (see head note)

3 tablespoons white balsamic vinegar

1 teaspoon Dijon mustard

1 tablespoon honey

pinch sea salt

¼ cup walnut oil

freshly ground black pepper

In a small skillet set over medium heat, toast the walnuts until they are golden and fragrant, about 8 minutes. Remove from heat and set aside. Place lettuce in a large salad bowl and toss with the fennel and onions. Prepare the apple and soak in a small bowl with 1 cup cold water and lemon juice. Place the prepared zucchini in a separate small bowl.

In another small bowl, stir together the white balsamic vinegar, mustard, honey, and sea salt. Slowly drizzle in the walnut oil, whisking to blend. Toss half of the vinaigrette with the lettuce mixture. Drain the apples and toss with the zucchini and the remaining vinaigrette. Mound the zucchini and apples on top of the lettuce. Garnish with walnuts and freshly ground pepper. ◇

## Apple Cabbage Slaw

*Apples and cabbage are a classic combination, and you can boost the nutrition quotient by adding kale and sunflower seeds. I prefer Lacinato kale, also known as dinosaur kale, but you can use any kale you like.* **SERVES 12**

4 cups shredded cabbage

2 cups shredded kale (see head note)

sea salt

¼ teaspoon celery seeds

1 teaspoon curry powder

¼ cup cider vinegar

6 tablespoons sunflower oil (Smude's) or canola oil

2 apples, cored and cut into matchsticks

¼ cup golden raisins

¼ cup minced Italian parsley

¼ cup sunflower seeds

freshly ground black pepper

In a large bowl, combine the cabbage and kale and sprinkle with 2 teaspoons salt. Place the mixture in a colander set over a bowl and let wilt for at least 1 hour. After it has wilted, place mixture in an ice-water bath to rinse. Drain mixture in a colander for about 30 minutes, then pat dry.

In a small bowl, mix together the celery seeds, curry powder, and cider vinegar. Slowly add the sunflower oil, whisking to blend.

In a large bowl, stir together the cabbage-kale mixture, dressing, apples, raisins, parsley, and sunflower seeds. Season with salt and pepper to taste. This makes a big batch and will keep in the fridge for up to 5 days. ◊

## Eve's Temptation

*Some debate whether Eve may have tempted Adam with a pomegranate instead of an apple. As much as I love pomegranates, they are not the easiest fruit to eat. An apple seems much more appealing in the heat of the moment. This salad keeps everyone happy with a tempting combination of both.* **SERVES 4**

1 (5-ounce) package mixed baby greens, rinsed and spun dry
2 medium apples (Cortland or Honeycrisp), cored and sliced
seeds from 1 pomegranate
1 bunch green onions, sliced
¼ cup chopped fresh mint
2 tablespoons pomegranate syrup (see tip)
2 tablespoons cider vinegar
1 clove garlic, minced
⅛ teaspoon sea salt
¼ cup extra-virgin olive oil
4 ounces MontAmore cheese (Sartori; see tip), shaved
¼ cup shelled pistachios
freshly ground black pepper

In a large salad bowl, mix together the greens, apples, pomegranate seeds, onions, and mint. In a small bowl, mix together the pomegranate syrup, cider vinegar, garlic, and salt. Slowly drizzle in the olive oil, whisking to blend. Toss the dressing with the salad, and garnish with MontAmore cheese, pistachios, and freshly ground black pepper to taste.

*Tip:* To make pomegranate syrup, simmer 1 cup pomegranate juice for about 45 minutes, until reduced by half. If MontAmore is not available, substitute a good-quality Parmesan. ◊

# CAESAR APPLE SALAD

*This salad represents an aha moment for me. The question was, "Can I put apples in everything?" Well, the answer is: just about. Many fresh-from-the-orchard apples work well in this combination, which has become one of my favorite "add apples to a classic salad" recipes. Try a Red Haralson or a Regent.* **SERVES 4**

**CROUTONS**

4 tablespoons (½ stick) butter, melted

1 clove garlic, minced

4 cups cubed ciabatta

**DRESSING**

1 large pasteurized egg

½ teaspoon Dijon mustard

3 anchovies (Wild Planet), mashed

1 clove garlic, minced

pinch sea salt

freshly ground black pepper

2 tablespoons freshly squeezed lemon juice

6 tablespoons extra-virgin olive oil

**SALAD**

1 head romaine, chopped, rinsed, and spun dry

1 red onion, sliced

2 medium apples, cored and sliced

⅓ cup freshly grated Parmesan (Carr Valley Canaria; see tip), plus 2 ounces shaved

salt and freshly ground black pepper

...........................

Preheat oven to 400 degrees. Stir together the melted butter and minced garlic in a small bowl. Place ciabatta cubes in a medium bowl and drizzle the butter and garlic over the top. Mix until all of the cubes are coated and the butter is well distributed. Spread the bread cubes onto a baking sheet and toast in the oven for 10 to 12 minutes, until golden. Remove and allow to cool.

For the dressing, in a small bowl stir together the egg, mustard, anchovies, garlic, salt, and several twists of freshly ground black pepper. Mix in the lemon juice. Slowly drizzle in the olive oil, whisking to blend.

In a large salad bowl, toss together the lettuce, onions, and apples. Add the dressing, grated Parmesan, and croutons and toss until all of the lettuce is coated. Garnish with shaved Parmesan, salt, and black pepper.

*Tip:* Canaria, from Wisconsin's Carr Valley Cheese Company, is a firm, Parmesan-like cheese made from sheep, goat, and cow milk. If you can't find Canaria, Sartori's BellaVitano is another great option from Wisconsin. Or use your favorite Parmesan. ◊

# APPLE MY HONEY SALAD

*This salad is a snap to put together. To make ahead, hold out the lettuce, toss together the remaining ingredients, refrigerate for up to four days, and then add the lettuce to serve.* **SERVES 6**

1 cup pepitas (pumpkin seeds) or sunflower seeds

1 tablespoon honey

1 tablespoon sunflower or canola oil

½ teaspoon Apple Spice Blend (page 15)

juice of 1 lemon

1 cup water

2 medium crisp, tart apples, cored and chopped

1 (15-ounce) can cannellini beans, rinsed and drained, or 2 cups cooked

2 ribs celery, sliced thin

1 small sweet onion, sliced thin

1 cup minced red bell pepper

1 head romaine, chopped, rinsed, and spun dry

3 tablespoons cider vinegar

2 tablespoons honey

1 teaspoon cinnamon

½ cup olive oil

½ cup chopped fresh mint

sea salt and freshly ground black pepper

In a small skillet set over medium-high heat, toast the pepitas for about 5 minutes. When they begin to brown, stir in the honey, oil, and spice blend until well coated. Spread the pepitas on a piece of parchment paper to cool.

In a medium bowl, mix lemon juice with water. Toss chopped apples in water and let sit for a few minutes, then drain. In a large bowl, mix together apples, beans, celery, onions, red pepper, and lettuce. In a small bowl, mix together cider vinegar, honey, and cinnamon. Slowly drizzle in the olive oil, whisking to blend. Add the vinaigrette to the salad and toss. Finish with pepitas and mint on top and a sprinkle of salt and a grind of pepper to garnish. ◊

## BEST HEART-HEALTHY SALAD

*This salad is so delectable and fetching to the eye, it's hard to believe it can keep the ticker happy, too. Garlic, radicchio, olive oil, beans, almonds, and of course apples are full of phytonutrients that promote heart health. Many types of apples will work beautifully. Seek out one with a crisp, sweet-tart flavor like Fireside or Honeycrisp.* **SERVES 4**

3 tablespoons cider vinegar

2 tablespoons honey

1 clove garlic, minced

1 teaspoon Dijon mustard

⅛ teaspoon salt

⅛ teaspoon freshly ground black pepper

¼ cup extra-virgin olive oil

8 leaves butter lettuce, rinsed and spun dry

½ head radicchio, cut into ribbons

½ cup sliced red onion

1 cup cooked or canned chickpeas

1 large apple (see head note), cored and sliced

¼ cup chopped almonds

½ cup chopped fresh mint

In a small bowl, mix together the cider vinegar, honey, garlic, mustard, salt, and pepper. Slowly drizzle in the olive oil, whisking to blend. Set aside.

Arrange 2 lettuce leaves on each of 4 salad plates. In a medium bowl, toss radicchio, onions, chickpeas, and apples. Add the vinaigrette to the salad mixture and gently toss to coat. Divide mixture among the 4 plates, mounding on top of the lettuce. Garnish with chopped almonds and mint.

*Tip:* For a champagne vinaigrette, swap in champagne vinegar for cider vinegar. ◊

## ENDIVE, APPLE, AND BIG WOODS BLUE SALAD

*Big Woods Blue is a farmstead sheep's milk cheese from Shepherd's Way Farm in southeastern Minnesota. The creamy and sharp cheese pairs beautifully with sweet and crisp SweeTango or Frostbite apples.* **SERVES 4**

- 1 cup hazelnuts (filberts)
- 1 teaspoon Dijon mustard
- 1 small shallot, minced
- ¼ teaspoon kosher salt
- 2 tablespoons unfermented grape juice (see tip)
- ¼ cup extra-virgin olive oil
- 2 heads Belgian endive, sliced lengthwise into matchsticks
- 2 medium apples (see head note), cored, halved, and cut into matchsticks
- 2 tablespoons chopped fresh tarragon
- 4 ounces blue cheese (Big Woods Blue), crumbled
- freshly ground black pepper

Preheat oven to 350 degrees. Spread out the hazelnuts in a small rimmed baking pan. Toast in the oven for 15 minutes, until fragrant. Pour the nuts onto a dish towel and roll it up. Set aside to cool for about 30 minutes. When cooled, rub the nuts in the towel to remove skins.

In a small bowl, stir together the mustard, shallot, salt, and grape juice. Slowly drizzle in the olive oil, whisking to blend. In a medium bowl, toss endive, apples, tarragon, and vinaigrette. Divide among 4 chilled salad plates. Sprinkle with blue cheese and hazelnuts. Grind fresh pepper on top.

*Tip:* Try Locust Lane Vineyards Verjus Blanc, a fresh, unfermented grape juice made from Minnesota-grown Frontenac gris grapes. You can substitute 1 tablespoon cider vinegar and 1 tablespoon lemon juice. ◊

## Harvest Apple Salad

*In need of a showstopper for an autumn get-together? This salad looks gorgeous mounded on a large platter but could also be composed on individual plates. Dress the components separately so that the red from the beets does not turn everything pink.* **SERVES 8**

2 medium beets

2 cups chopped butternut squash

¾ cup plus 1 tablespoon extra-virgin olive oil

¼ cup cider vinegar

1 shallot, minced

1 teaspoon Dijon mustard

1 teaspoon honey

½ teaspoon Apple Spice Blend (page 15)

pinch sea salt

freshly ground black pepper

1 head butter lettuce, rinsed and torn into pieces

1 cup cooked wild rice

2 large apples (SweeTango), cored and chopped

¼ cup chopped walnuts, toasted

8 ounces goat cheese (Stickney Hills or Singing Hills Dairy), crumbled

Preheat oven to 400 degrees. Scrub beets and wrap in aluminum foil. Toss squash with 1 tablespoon olive oil and spread onto a baking sheet. Roast beets and squash for 30 minutes or until tender. Allow to cool; when beets are cool, remove skin with the back of a spoon, then dice and set aside.

For the vinaigrette, in a small bowl whisk together cider vinegar, shallot, mustard, honey, spice blend, salt, and a few twists of black pepper. Slowly drizzle in remaining ¾ cup olive oil, whisking to blend.

Place lettuce and wild rice in a large bowl and toss with ¼ cup of vinaigrette. Mound the lettuce-rice mixture on a large platter. In 3 separate bowls, toss beets, squash, and apples with vinaigrette to lightly coat. Add each component as a layer atop the lettuce. Garnish with walnuts and goat cheese.  ◊

## MIDWESTERN COBB

*The Cobb salad originated in the 1930s at the Hollywood Brown Derby in Lake Buena Vista, Florida, and was named after the owner, Robert Cobb. It is a composed salad with a few must-have ingredients. In this rendition, I have substituted apples for the tomatoes. Choose any fresh apple that is sweet or tart but firm.* **SERVES 4**

8 slices applewood-smoked bacon (see tip)

4 large eggs (organic preferred)

2 tablespoons red wine vinegar (see tip)

1 teaspoon Dijon mustard

1 clove garlic, minced

¼ teaspoon sea salt

¼ cup sunflower oil (Smude's) or canola oil

1 head romaine, chopped, rinsed, and spun dry (8 cups)

2 cups shredded rotisserie chicken

1 cup crumbled blue cheese (AmaBlu St. Pete's Select; see tip)

½ cup snipped fresh chives

2 medium apples, cored and chopped

1 avocado, peeled and chopped

1 cup cooked or canned chickpeas

¼ cup salted sunflower seeds, toasted

freshly ground black pepper

Preheat oven to 400 degrees. Place a cooling rack on a rimmed baking sheet. Lay the bacon on the rack. Roast for about 18 minutes, until crispy and golden brown. When cool, chop and set aside.

Place the eggs in a small saucepan and cover with water. Set over high heat. When the water begins to boil, turn off the heat, cover the pan, and let sit for 10 minutes. Pour off the hot water and rinse eggs with cold water to stop the cooking. Peel, chop, and set aside.

In a small bowl, whisk together the red wine vinegar, mustard, garlic, and salt. Slowly add the sunflower oil, whisking to blend.

Place 2 cups of chopped romaine in each of 4 serving bowls. Layer each of the remaining salad components—chicken, cheese, chives, apples, avocado, chickpeas, bacon, eggs, sunflower seeds—in rows. Finish by drizzling the dressing on top and garnishing with freshly ground pepper.

*Tips:* Excellent options for midwestern applewood bacon include Nueske's from Wisconsin and the Lunds and Byerly's brand. AmaBlu "St. Pete's Select" is from the Caves of Faribault cheese company in Minnesota. Try Locust Lane Vineyards Verjus Rouge, an unfermented grape must juice, in place of vinegar. ◊

# SweeTango Arugula Fennel Salad

*Playing upon the Latin reference to "tango," this Spanish-inspired salad has a midwestern twist. The SweeTango apple is the star, but other sweet-tart apples can stand in if necessary. Both sherry vinegar and Marcona almonds are from Spain, but instead of Manchego, a Spanish sheep's milk cheese, I recommend using Roth GranQueso, a Wisconsin cow's milk cheese that was inspired by Manchego.* **SERVES 4**

- 2  apples (SweeTango), cored, halved, and cut into matchsticks
- 1  bulb fennel, sliced thin
- 4  ounces Manchego (Roth GranQueso) or Parmesan, cut into matchsticks
- 1  (5-ounce) package baby arugula, rinsed and spun dry
- 2  tablespoons sherry vinegar
- ⅛  teaspoon sea salt
- 1  teaspoon honey
- 1  clove garlic, minced
- ¼  cup extra-virgin olive oil
-    freshly ground black pepper
- 1  bunch Italian parsley (see tip), chopped
- ¼  cup Marcona almonds (see tip)

In a large salad bowl, stir together apples, fennel, cheese, and arugula. In a small bowl, stir together sherry vinegar, salt, honey, and garlic. Slowly drizzle in the olive oil, whisking to blend. Add the vinaigrette to the salad and toss. Garnish with freshly ground pepper, parsley, and almonds.

*Tips:* Red Rambo Micro-greens from Morning Sun Farms can take the place of the Italian parsley. For the Marcona almonds you can substitute blanched almonds that have been toasted in a small skillet until golden and tossed with a little olive oil and sea salt.  ◇

# TABBOULEH ALLA APPLE

*A Middle Eastern dish, tabbouleh is usually made with bulgur wheat, cucumbers, and lots of parsley. This gluten-free twist swaps in quinoa and apples. Quinoa, a seed from the goosefoot grain grown in the Andes of South America, contains essential amino acids and is high in protein. Serve this dish with pita bread and hummus.* **SERVES 8**

      1  cup rainbow or regular quinoa
      2  medium firm, sweet apples, cored and minced
  1¼  cups minced fresh parsley
   ½  cup minced fresh mint
      1  bunch green onions, sliced
         juice of 1 lemon
   ¼  cup extra-virgin olive oil
         sea salt and freshly ground black pepper

Rinse the quinoa in a colander until the water runs clear. In a medium saucepan set over high heat, bring 2 cups of water to a boil. Stir in the quinoa, reduce heat, cover, and cook for about 15 minutes. The grains should look like they have expanded and opened. Drain if necessary and let cool.

Combine apples, parsley, mint, and onions in a large bowl. Stir in the cooled quinoa, lemon juice, and olive oil and sprinkle in salt and pepper to taste.  ◊

## HONEYGOLD CURRY TUNA SALAD

*This salad, developed for my gourmet deli, the Rosebud Grocery at St. Anthony Main in Minneapolis, quickly became a favorite, and we had to have it in the display case every week. The mixture of savory and sweet keeps you coming back for more. It is great on its own or served on a bed of greens or as a sandwich filling in your favorite croissant or whole-grain bun.* **SERVES 4**

- 2 medium apples (Honeygold), cored and chopped
- 2 ribs celery, chopped
- 1 bunch green onions, sliced
- 2 (5-ounce) cans top-quality albacore tuna, drained
- ⅔ cup golden raisins
- 2 tablespoons freshly squeezed lemon juice
- ¼ cup mayonnaise
- ¼ cup Greek-style yogurt
- 1 tablespoon curry powder
- salt and freshly ground black pepper
- 2 tablespoons sliced almonds

In a large bowl, stir together apples, celery, onions, tuna, and raisins. In a small bowl, mix together lemon juice, mayonnaise, yogurt, curry powder, and a sprinkle of salt and pepper, stirring until blended. Toss the dressing with the apple-tuna mixture until coated. Taste and adjust for seasoning. Garnish with sliced almonds.  ◇

## Cavatappi Pasta Apple Salad

*Cavatappi (corkscrew-shaped) pasta is genius when used in pasta salads. The only thing that can improve these salads is to add apples. The apple you choose should have a crisp texture but can be sweet or tart or a combination of both. SnowSweet, with its sweet-tart and savory flavor, is especially well suited to this recipe because its crisp flesh stays snowy white.* **SERVES 8**

- 1 (16-ounce) box cavatappi pasta
- ¼ cup plus 2 tablespoons extra-virgin olive oil
- 2 medium apples (see head note), cored and sliced
- ½ cup chopped red onion
- 1 red bell pepper, chopped
- ½ cup chopped sun dried tomatoes in oil
- 2 cups shredded rotisserie chicken
- 4 ounces premium Parmesan (Sartori Reserve BellaVitano Gold), coarsely shredded

1 clove garlic, minced

1 teaspoon Dijon mustard

¼ teaspoon sea salt

1 tablespoon white balsamic vinegar

freshly ground black pepper

¼ cup pine nuts, toasted

¼ cup chopped fresh parsley

¼ cup chopped fresh basil

..........................

Cook the cavatappi pasta al dente according to package directions. Drain and rinse with cold water. In a large salad bowl, toss the pasta with 2 tablespoons olive oil. Add the apples, onions, bell pepper, tomatoes, chicken, and Parmesan. In a small bowl, mix together garlic, mustard, salt, and white balsamic vinegar. Slowly drizzle in the remaining ¼ cup olive oil, whisking to blend. Toss the vinaigrette with the pasta salad until well coated. Garnish with freshly ground pepper, pine nuts, parsley, and basil.  ◇

## Wild Rice, Lentil, and Orzo Salad with Curried Vinaigrette

*Wild rice, lentils, and orzo along with a good amount of spice provide earthy flavors and textures to this complex salad. A firm, crisp apple adds just the right amount of sweet and crunch to balance all the spice. This recipe makes a big batch perfect for sharing. Let it sit for a day to let all the flavors mingle.*

**SERVES 12**

1 cup wild rice, rinsed

2 teaspoons sea salt, divided

1½ cups brown lentils

1 (16-ounce) package orzo

⅔ cup slivered almonds

2 large apples, cored and chopped

½ cup chopped sweet onion

1 teaspoon curry powder

1 teaspoon Apple Spice Blend (page 15)

½ teaspoon smoked paprika

¼ teaspoon red pepper flakes

1 teaspoon kosher salt

2 cloves garlic, minced

2 teaspoons Dijon mustard

½ cup cider vinegar

1 cup olive oil

In a medium saucepan, combine wild rice, 6 cups water, and 1 teaspoon sea salt; cook over medium heat for about 45 minutes. Drain and rinse with cold water. In a separate saucepan, combine lentils with 2 cups water; cook over medium heat for about 25 minutes, until tender. Drain and rinse with cold water. In another saucepan, bring 8 cups water and remaining teaspoon sea salt to a boil. Add the orzo and cook for about 8 minutes, until al dente. Drain and rinse with cold water. In a small skillet set over medium-high heat, toast the almonds until golden brown, about 5 minutes. Toss the wild rice, lentils, and orzo in a large bowl with the apples, onions, and almonds. Set aside.

To make the vinaigrette, whisk together curry powder, spice blend, paprika, red pepper flakes, and salt. Stir in garlic, mustard, and cider vinegar. Slowly drizzle in the olive oil, whisking to blend. Toss vinaigrette with salad. Let sit, refrigerated, for at least 1 hour to allow the flavors to develop. ◊

SIDES

S ide dishes: the unsung heroes of the dinner plate. You wouldn't serve a pork chop or a fish fillet without a little window dressing to complete the picture. Think of a beautiful roasted turkey at Thanksgiving; it would be lonely without all the side dishes to underpin the meal. If we are lucky, there are leftovers of those sides to be enjoyed as a late-night snack or light lunch. The versatile dishes collected here are delicious "on the side" but complex enough to shine on their own. Apples accentuate the earthy flavors of the autumn season.

## YUMMY APPLE YAMS

*Yams are full of beta carotene and apples are brimming with fiber, vitamins, and antioxidants. How can something so packed with nutrition be so yummy too?* SERVES 8

- 2 yams, peeled and spiralized or sliced thin
- 2 pounds apples, cored and spiralized or sliced thin
- 1 onion, sliced thin
- 2 tablespoons olive oil
- pinch salt
- pinch black pepper
- 1 tablespoon chopped fresh rosemary
- ⅓ cup honey
- 4 tablespoons (½ stick) butter, melted

Preheat oven to 500 degrees. In a large bowl, mix together the yams, apples, onions, olive oil, salt, pepper, and rosemary. Spread mixture onto a rimmed baking sheet and bake for about 30 minutes, until golden brown and tender. Scrape mixture into a large serving bowl. Stir together the honey and butter and drizzle over the yammy apples. ◊

## Apple-Walnut Stuffing

*Apple harvest season is the best time of year for big family get-togethers where comfort food takes center stage. What would Thanksgiving be without stuffing? Use leftovers on a turkey sandwich or as a side with roasted chicken.* **SERVES 10–12**

8 cups cubed ciabatta

1 pound pork sausage (see tip)

8 tablespoons (1 stick) butter

3 ribs celery, chopped

1 large leek, rinsed and sliced

4 cups chopped Haralson or other red apple

1 cup chicken broth

1 cup apple cider

½ teaspoon red pepper flakes, crushed

1 cup chopped walnuts

1 cup cooked wild rice

1 tablespoon minced fresh sage

1 teaspoon minced fresh rosemary

½ teaspoon kosher salt

freshly ground black pepper

1 cup shredded sharp Cheddar (see tip)

Preheat oven to 350 degrees. Grease a 9x13–inch baking dish and set aside. Place bread cubes in a large bowl and set aside. Set a large skillet over medium-high heat. Add sausage to the pan and cook, stirring to break it into small pieces, for about 8 minutes, until no longer pink. Drain meat and set aside. Melt butter in the skillet and add the celery, leeks, and apples. Cook, stirring frequently, until soft, about 10 minutes. Stir in the broth, cider, red pepper flakes, walnuts, wild rice, sage, rosemary, salt, and 3 to 4 twists of pepper. Add to the bowl with the bread cubes, stirring to combine, and then mix in the sausage and cheese. Spoon stuffing mixture into prepared pan and cover with aluminum foil. Bake for 20 minutes, then remove foil and bake for about 12 more minutes, until the bread turns golden brown.

*Tip:* My favorite pork sausage for this recipe is Woodend Farm from Greggwood Farm in St. Bonifacius, Minnesota. It's higher in fat, which is what makes it so good. For the cheese, I like to use Widmer's Cheddar from Wisconsin. ◊

## Roasted Apples and Roots

*Oven roasting brings out all of the best, luscious, earthy flavors in these root vegetables, while the apple adds a supple lift. Chop all of the pieces into about the same size chunks so that they will cook at the same rate.* **SERVES 8**

2 apples, cored and chopped

1 red onion, sliced

1 yam, peeled and chopped

4 parsnips, sliced

2 rutabagas, peeled and chopped

4 turnips, peeled and sliced

¼ cup cider vinegar

2 tablespoons sunflower or canola oil

½ teaspoon salt

½ teaspoon freshly ground black pepper

6 cloves garlic, peeled and halved

2 tablespoons chopped fresh rosemary

Preheat oven to 425 degrees. In a large bowl, stir together apples and vegetables (onion through turnips). Drizzle in the cider vinegar and sunflower oil and sprinkle on the salt and pepper, tossing to combine. Spread mixture onto a rimmed baking sheet, and roast for 30 minutes. Stir in the garlic and rosemary, and continue to roast for another 15 minutes, until golden brown and tender. ◊

## MOROCCAN APPLES AND SWISS CHARD

*I love the rich, warm flavor of Moroccan spices. Moroccan cooking often melds savory with sweet flavors, and in this dish apples contribute a spot-on sweetness. Serve with salmon, chicken, or pork.* **SERVES 6**

3 tablespoons extra-virgin olive oil

1 bunch red Swiss chard, stems cut into matchsticks and leaves chopped (about 8 cups)

1 cup chopped onion

2 cloves garlic, minced

2 apples, cored and chopped

2 teaspoons Ras el Hanout (page 17)

sea salt and freshly ground black pepper

Set a large skillet over medium-high heat and add olive oil. When the oil is starting to shimmer, add the chard stems and onions. Cook, stirring, for about 5 minutes. Add the chard leaves, garlic, apples, seasoning, and a sprinkle of salt and pepper. Cook, stirring, for about 10 minutes, until wilted. Taste and adjust seasonings if necessary. ◊

# Red Rice with Roasted Apples and Brussels Sprouts

*Not only is this dish tasty and pretty, it is good for you, too. Roasting the apples with the Brussels sprouts and onions brings out a deep, rich, sweet flavor and makes a wonderful side dish for chicken, pork, or beef. If you are lucky enough to have leftovers, this combination is also delicious tossed with greens for a salad.* **SERVES 6**

......................

4 ounces thinly sliced pancetta

1 cup sliced almonds

1 cup red rice, or substitute brown rice

sea salt

1 pound Brussels sprouts, trimmed and sliced

2 apples, cored and chopped

1 medium onion, chopped

2 tablespoons extra-virgin olive oil

freshly ground black pepper

¼ cup chopped Italian parsley

......................

In a skillet set over medium-high heat, fry pancetta until crispy. Drain on a paper towel. When cool enough to handle, chop and set aside. In a small skillet set over medium heat, toast almonds until golden brown. Set aside.

In a medium saucepan, bring 2 cups of water to a boil. Add the red rice and ¼ teaspoon sea salt; reduce heat and simmer for about 20 minutes, until tender. Drain if necessary and set aside.

Preheat oven to 425 degrees. In a large bowl, toss Brussels sprouts, apples, and onions with olive oil and a sprinkle of salt and pepper. Spread in a single layer on a rimmed baking sheet, and roast for about 30 minutes, stirring after 15 minutes. In a serving bowl, toss mixture with red rice, almonds, and parsley. Taste and adjust seasonings if necessary. Garnish with pancetta. ◊

# Roasted Apples with Sage and Fingerling Potatoes

*Fingerling potatoes, available in purple, red, and yellow, are a heritage cultivar that grows long and knobby. Their creamy texture and fun shape team up with apples for this savory dish, appealing served with pork, chicken, turkey, or beef.* **SERVES 8**

..........................

1 sweet onion, chopped

2 apples, cored and chopped

zest and juice of 1 lemon

2 pounds fingerling potatoes, scrubbed and halved

3 tablespoons olive oil

4 tablespoons (½ stick) butter, melted

6 cloves garlic, peeled

½ teaspoon sea salt

½ teaspoon freshly ground black pepper

2 tablespoons fresh sage cut into ribbons

..........................

Preheat oven to 425 degrees. In a large bowl, toss together the onions, apples, lemon zest and juice, potatoes, olive oil, butter, garlic, salt, and pepper. Spread mixture onto a rimmed baking sheet and roast for 15 minutes. Stir in the sage and continue to cook for another 15 minutes, until golden brown. ◇

# SOUPS *and* SANDWICHES

he moment there's a chill in the air it's as if a switch goes on and we crave comfort food. What could be cozier than a pot of soup simmering on the stove? Nestled alongside the soup, a sandwich finds its customary place. Laced with apples, these dishes are just another way to enjoy the flavors of the season.

## HEARTY CABBAGE APPLE SOUP

*Another name for this dish could be Healing Hearty Soup. Amped up on good-for-you ingredients, it offers homey comfort. With ham, cabbage, parsnips, and caraway seeds, this recipe gives a nod to Germany's strong apple traditions. Choose a firm, tart apple such as Haralson or Regent. This soup is excellent with artisanal rye bread.* **SERVES 10**

- 2 tablespoons canola oil
- 8 ounces thick-sliced smoked ham, chopped
- 1 cup chopped yellow onion
- 1 rib celery, chopped
- 2 carrots, peeled and chopped
- 2 parsnips, peeled and chopped
- 2 medium firm, tart apples, cored and chopped
- ¼ cup apple brandy
- 4 cups chopped cabbage
- 4 cups chicken broth
- ½ teaspoon salt
- ½ teaspoon freshly ground black pepper
- ½ teaspoon caraway seed
- 1 teaspoon fennel seed

In a large Dutch oven set over medium heat, warm canola oil. Add ham and cook for a few minutes. Add the onions, celery, and carrots and cook, stirring occasionally, until onions are soft and translucent, about 10 minutes. Add the parsnips and apples and cook, stirring occasionally, for 5 minutes. Pour in the apple brandy and cook to reduce the liquid, scraping the bottom of the pan to loosen any browned bits. Stir in the cabbage, broth, and seasonings. Bring to a simmer and cook for 30 minutes. Serve in warmed soup bowls. ◇

## Roasted Pumpkin Apple Soup

*It's hard not to just use the versatile and delicious Honeycrisp all the time. I sometimes feel like I'm slighting the other available apples. Go ahead and substitute any firm, sweet-tart apple you like in this lovely starter.* **SERVES 10**

1 (2-pound) baking pumpkin, quartered and seeded

4 tablespoons extra-virgin olive oil, divided

sea salt and freshly ground black pepper

1½ pounds apples (see head note), cored and chopped, plus 1 for garnish

2 carrots, peeled and chopped

3 small shallots, chopped

1 rib celery, chopped

2 cloves garlic, minced

1 tablespoon minced fresh sage

½ teaspoon grated nutmeg

4 cups chicken stock

2 cups apple cider

¼ cup honey

1 tablespoon pepitas (pumpkin seeds), or substitute sunflower seeds

2 tablespoons pumpkin seed oil, or substitute walnut or olive oil

Preheat oven to 425 degrees. Drizzle the pumpkin quarters with 1 tablespoon olive oil and season with salt and pepper. Lay cut-side down on a rimmed baking sheet. Roast for about 45 minutes. As the pumpkin is roasting, core and slice the garnish apple into 20 thin slices. Toss with 1 tablespoon olive oil and lay on a baking sheet lined with parchment paper. Roast for about 15 minutes, until golden. Allow to cool. When the pumpkin is tender, set aside to cool. Scoop out the flesh.

Meanwhile, in a large stockpot set over medium-high heat, warm remaining 2 tablespoons olive oil. Add the carrots, shallots, celery, chopped apples, and a pinch of salt and pepper. Cover and cook for about 10 minutes, stirring occasionally. When the vegetables and apples are beginning to soften, add the garlic, sage, and nutmeg. Stir for about 1 minute, until garlic is fragrant. Stir in the pumpkin, stock, and cider, cover the pot, and bring to a boil. Reduce heat to medium low and simmer for about 15 minutes. Stir in the honey.

Using an immersion blender, puree the soup until smooth. (Alternatively, work in batches to carefully puree the soup in a blender.) Taste and adjust seasonings if necessary. Serve in warmed soup bowls. Garnish each serving with 2 slices of roasted apple, a pinch of pepitas, and a drizzle of pumpkin seed oil.  ◊

## Smoky Cheddar Apple Soup

*I like to think of this as a more sophisticated cousin to beer cheese soup. Using apple-smoked bacon, smoked Cheddar, and smoked paprika makes for a triple-good treat. Apples fresh from the orchard tie it all together. Serve with crusty artisanal whole grain bread.* **SERVES 10**

..........................

- 4 slices applewood-smoked bacon, chopped
- 1 cup chopped sweet white onion
- 1 carrot, peeled and chopped
- 1 rib celery, chopped
- 1 clove garlic, minced
- 2 medium apples, cored and chopped
- 1 cup apple cider, or substitute apple wine or hard cider
- 8 tablespoons (1 stick) butter, cut into pieces
- ½ cup Wondra or all-purpose flour
- 4 cups low-sodium chicken stock
- 4 cups whole milk (organic preferred)
- 12 ounces smoked Cheddar (Carr Valley), shredded
- ¼ teaspoon cayenne
- ½ teaspoon smoked paprika
- ½ teaspoon sea salt

..........................

Set a large Dutch oven over medium heat. Add the bacon and cook until brown and crispy. Add the onions, carrot, celery, garlic, and apples. Cook, stirring, until vegetables and apples are soft and onions are translucent, about 15 minutes. Pour in the cider and cook to reduce the liquid by half, scraping the bottom of the pan to loosen any browned bits. Using an immersion blender, puree soup until smooth. (Alternatively, work in batches to carefully puree the soup in a blender. Then return soup to the pot.) Push puree to the sides of the pot and add the butter and flour to the center. Cook, stirring, until the flour browns, about 5 minutes. Whisk in the stock and whole milk and bring to a simmer. Slowly stir in the cheese until melted. Season with cayenne, smoked paprika, and salt. Ladle into warmed soup bowls for serving.  ◇

## White Bean, Kale, and Apple Soup

*This soup has its feet firmly planted in Tuscany, where people pride them-selves on being called "bean eaters." White beans are a favorite; cannellini or white navy will work nicely. Pancetta is an Italian uncured rolled bacon with a distinctive salty flavor. Wonderful midwestern-produced pancettas are available from Red Table Meat Company and La Quercia.* **SERVES 8**

1 tablespoon olive oil

4 ounces pancetta, chopped

1 cup chopped sweet white onion

1 rib celery, minced

1 shallot, minced

1 large apple, cored and chopped

1 teaspoon minced fresh oregano

½ cup hard cider (see tip)

1 (15-ounce) can white beans, rinsed and drained, or 2 cups cooked

4 cups chopped kale

- 4 cups chicken stock
- ¼ teaspoon crushed red pepper flakes
- ½ teaspoon sea salt
- ¼ teaspoon freshly ground black pepper
- ¼ cup chopped Italian parsley
- ¼ cup chopped fresh basil

Set a large Dutch oven over medium heat. Add olive oil and pancetta and cook, stirring, for about 5 minutes. Remove pancetta and drain on a paper towel–lined plate. Add the onions, celery, shallot, and apple and cook, stirring, until translucent and tender. Stir in the oregano, pour in the hard cider, and cook to reduce the liquid, scraping the bottom of the pan to loosen any browned bits. Add the beans, kale, stock, red pepper flakes, salt, and pepper. Bring to a simmer and cook for at least 20 minutes. When ready to serve, ladle into warmed soup bowls and garnish with pancetta, parsley, and basil.

*Tip:* Many varieties of hard cider, or fermented apple cider, are available at liquor stores. For a special treat, pick up hard cider from Sociable Cider Werks in Minneapolis and enjoy a glass with your soup. ◊

## Tarragon Chicken Apple Salad Sandwich

*The combination of tarragon and apple is magical. I can't think of any fresh orchard apple that wouldn't work in this recipe. My preference would be for a firm, crisp texture, but tart or sweet is up to you.* **SERVES 4**

............................

- 2 cups chopped rotisserie chicken
- ¼ cup minced sweet onion
- 1 rib celery, minced
- 2 cups minced apple
- 2 tablespoons raw unsalted pepitas (pumpkin seeds) or sunflower seeds
- 1 tablespoon dried tarragon, crushed
- ½ cup mayonnaise
- ½ cup Greek-style yogurt
- sea salt and freshly ground black pepper
- 8 slices artisanal bread
- 4 leaves butter lettuce

............................

In a medium bowl, mix together chicken, onions, celery, apples, and pepitas. Stir in the tarragon, mayonnaise, and yogurt. Season with salt and pepper to taste. Spread mixture evenly over 4 slices of bread. Top each with a lettuce leaf and a slice of bread. Cut in half to serve.

*Tip:* Skip the bread and mound a scoop of the salad on top of a bed of mixed greens. ◊

## Apple Avocado Tuna Salad Sandwich

*Many fresh orchard apples will work well in this new version of the classic tuna salad sandwich. I prefer a firm or crisp texture, but for flavor, sweet and tart are both fine. La Crescent, McIntosh, Regent, SnowSweet, and Frostbite are all delicious. Serve the sandwiches with apple slices and kale chips.* **SERVES 4**

1 large apple, cored and minced

½ cup minced red onion

1 rib celery, minced

zest and juice of 1 lemon

1 (5-ounce) can tuna (Wild Planet), undrained

1 tablespoon olive oil

pinch sea salt

freshly ground black pepper

2 avocados

8 slices sourdough bread, lightly toasted

1 cup tightly packed baby greens

In a medium bowl, mix together the apple, onions, celery, lemon zest, half the lemon juice, and undrained tuna. Stir in the olive oil, salt, and pepper to taste. Peel and pit the avocados. In a small bowl, mash the avocado flesh with the remaining lemon juice. Spread each slice of bread with the avocado. Top 4 slices of bread with the tuna salad. Sprinkle baby greens on top of the salad. Cover with remaining bread slices.

*Tip:* If you would like to go *sans* bread, serve salad on butter lettuce leaves for a lettuce wrap. ◇

## Apple Panini

*Panini sandwiches make for a quick and easy dinner. Just add a cup of soup and an* insalata verde *(mixed green salad), and you will be all set. Don't forget a nice glass of Sangiovese.* **SERVES 4**

8  slices whole-grain sourdough bread

2  tablespoons olive oil

1  clove garlic, minced

¼  cup pesto sauce

4  ounces high-quality hard salami (Vecchio; see tip), sliced thin

8  ounces fontina (BelGioioso), shredded

1  apple (Wealthy or Red Baron), cored and minced

sea salt and freshly ground black pepper

Heat a panini grill or skillet to medium-high heat. Brush one side of each bread slice with olive oil and set oil-side down on a baking sheet. Stir garlic into the prepared pesto. Slather the inside of the bread slices with the pesto sauce. Add a layer of salami to 4 of the slices. Mix the cheese with the apple. Spoon the cheese and apple mixture on top of the salami. Press remaining 4 slices of bread on top to make sandwiches. Grill each sandwich for about 5 minutes, until golden and the cheese is melted. Sprinkle with sea salt and freshly ground pepper. Slice in half diagonally to serve.

*Tip:* I recommend the Vecchio Salami from Red Table Meat Company in Minneapolis, but you can substitute another high-quality hard salami. ◇

## ULTIMATE GRILLED APPLE CHEESE

*Grilled cheese sustained me through my college years. This is my favorite grown-up rendition, comfort food through and through. The mayonnaise trick comes from Gabrielle Hamilton, owner of Prune Restaurant in New York City. This recipe doubles easily for a crowd.* **SERVES 4**

........................

8 slices applewood-smoked bacon

½ cup mayonnaise

8 slices artisanal multigrain bread

8 ounces sharp Cheddar (Widmer's), shredded

2 crisp, tart apples, cored and sliced thin

sea salt

honey mustard

........................

Preheat oven to 400 degrees. Set a cooling rack on a rimmed baking sheet. Lay the bacon slices on the rack and roast for about 18 minutes, until crispy. When bacon is cool enough to handle, chop and set aside. Reduce oven temperature to 300 degrees.

Spread mayonnaise on each slice of bread and set aside, mayo-side down, on a baking sheet. In a medium bowl, mix together the bacon and the cheese. Layer apples on 4 slices of bread, then mound a scoop of bacon-cheese mixture on each. Cover with another slice of bread, mayo-side up.

Set a large, nonstick pan over medium heat. Fry each sandwich for about 5 minutes, then flip and fry for another 5 minutes. Keep sandwiches warm in the oven until ready to serve. Cut diagonally and sprinkle each with a little sea salt. Serve with a spoonful of mustard for dipping. ◇

## Apple Rollup

*Almond butter with julienned apples for a bit of sweet makes for an elegant riff on the original comfort food, peanut butter and jelly.* **SERVES 4**

........................

    4   (10-inch) whole wheat tortillas
    ¼   cup almond butter
    1   teaspoon Apple Spice Blend (page 15)
    1   apple, cored and cut into matchsticks
    1   cup baby arugula
    2   ounces sheep's milk cheese (Shepherd's Way), shredded
    2   tablespoons chopped smoked almonds

........................

Spread each tortilla with almond butter. Sprinkle with spice blend. Divide apples, arugula, cheese, and almonds among the tortillas. Fold in each side and then, starting at the edge closest to you, tightly roll up the tortilla. Cut on the diagonal. ◇

## APPLES AND BRUSSELS SPROUTS IN A POCKET

*Oven-roasting apples, Brussels sprouts, and onions unlocks their natural deep, sweet flavors. A sweet-tart, firm-textured apple, like the Regent, Zestar, or Keepsake, is best.* **SERVES 4**

2 medium apples, cored and chopped

2 cups thinly sliced Brussels sprouts

1 cup sliced red onion

2 teaspoons Ras el Hanout (page 17)

¼ teaspoon sea salt

2 tablespoons olive oil

2 tablespoons balsamic vinegar

1 cup cooked or canned chickpeas

4 whole wheat pita breads

Preheat oven to 400 degrees. In a medium bowl, toss together apples, Brussels sprouts, onions, seasoning, salt, olive oil, balsamic vinegar, and chickpeas. Spread onto a baking sheet and roast for about 20 minutes, stirring after the first 10 minutes. Let cool to room temperature. Cut pita breads in half, and spoon mixture into each pocket. ◊

# Thai Apple Chicken Burger

*In the taste profile for Thai cuisine, complex layers combine savory and spicy with a smattering of beautiful colors for eye appeal. Apples lend a lovely crunch and sweet flavor.* **SERVES 4**

**MAYONNAISE**

1 tablespoon sesame oil

½ cup minced apple

1 tablespoon Thai red curry paste

1½ teaspoons chopped fresh ginger

1 cup mayonnaise

**SLAW**

2 cups Chinese cabbage cut into matchsticks

¼ cup diagonally sliced green onion

1 cup apple cut into matchsticks

¼ cup chopped cilantro

1 tablespoon hoisin sauce

1 tablespoon sesame oil

juice of 1 lime

1 teaspoon rice wine vinegar

**BURGERS**

1 pound ground chicken

1 cup minced apple

1 tablespoon sambal oelek (Asian chili sauce) or Sriracha

1 clove garlic, minced

1 tablespoon chopped fresh ginger

1 tablespoon hoisin sauce

1½ teaspoons rice wine vinegar

½ cup chopped cilantro

2 tablespoons canola oil

4 sesame hamburger buns

..............................

To make the mayonnaise, in a small skillet, warm sesame oil over medium-high heat. Add apple and curry paste and cook, stirring, for about 3 minutes. Allow mixture to cool, then stir in ginger and mayonnaise. Refrigerate until ready to serve.

For the slaw, in a medium bowl, mix together the cabbage, onion, apple, and cilantro. In a small bowl, stir together hoisin sauce, sesame oil, lime juice, and rice wine vinegar. Pour into bowl with slaw ingredients and toss until evenly coated. Set aside.

Gently mix together burger ingredients (chicken through cilantro) until combined. Divide mixture into 4 portions and shape into patties. Preheat grill to high, about 400 degrees, and brush grates with canola oil (see tip). Grill the chicken patties for about 5 minutes without moving them to allow for a good sear so they do not fall apart. Carefully flip the burgers and grill for another 5 minutes, until internal temperature registers 165 degrees on a meat thermometer. Toast the buns.

To assemble the sandwich, generously spread the top and bottom buns with mayonnaise. Place the grilled burger on the bottom bun and top with ½ cup of slaw. Lean the top bun against the burger for a nice presentation.

*Tip:* You can also attain wonderful results using this method with a stovetop grill pan. ◇

## APPLE PORK SLIDERS

*Along with apple season, fall is football season, prime time for delicious snacking. This easy sandwich is also pretty tidy. Roasting the onions and apples brings out their rich, complex flavor.* **MAKES 24 SMALL SANDWICHES**

- 2 pounds pork tenderloin
- 3 tablespoons olive oil, divided
- ½ teaspoon cinnamon
- ½ teaspoon smoked paprika
- ¼ teaspoon cayenne
- sea salt and freshly ground black pepper
- 1 large red onion, sliced
- 2 apples (SnowSweet), cored and sliced
- ¼ cup balsamic vinegar
- 24 Hawaiian sweet rolls
- 1 (4.5-ounce) package goat cheese (Snøfrisk; see tip), at room temperature

Preheat oven to 425 degrees. Rub the pork with 1 tablespoon olive oil. Mix cinnamon, paprika, cayenne, ½ teaspoon sea salt, and ½ teaspoon pepper together in a small bowl. Sprinkle pork with spices and rub in; place on a rimmed baking sheet. Roast pork about 20 minutes, until internal temperature registers 145 degrees on a meat thermometer. Remove from oven, tent with foil, and let rest for at least 10 minutes. Cut into ¼-inch slices.

In a bowl, toss together the onions, apples, balsamic vinegar, and remaining 2 tablespoons olive oil. On a rimmed baking sheet lined with parchment paper, spread mixture in a single layer. Sprinkle with salt and pepper. Roast for 10 minutes, stir, and roast for another 10 minutes.

Open each roll and spread with goat cheese. Add a slice of pork and a spoonful of roasted onion-apple mixture to each slider.

*Tip:* Snøfrisk is a mild, creamy goat cheese from Norway.  ◊

# MAINS

W hen it comes to the main course, apples play a supporting role, but what an exciting role it is. Complementing the succulent center of the plate with exquisite pops of color and bright flavor, apples bring much enjoyment to a meal. Whether in a sauce or as a stuffing, apples pair extremely well with everything from pork to poultry to seafood. Choose a firm variety that will retain its toothsome quality when cooked.

## SAVORY SWEET SIXTEEN APPLE FOCACCIA

*The name for* focaccia, *the oily round rustic Italian bread used for thick-crust pizza, means "to bake on the hearth," referring to the scrap of bread used to check to see if a wood-burning oven was hot enough to bake bread. The multiple risings are extra work, but the results are amazing. For a short-cut, use fresh pizza dough from the deli or dairy department. The Sweet Sixteen apple is my favorite, but you could also try McIntosh or Connell Red.*

**SERVES 6**

**DOUGH**

- 6 cups unbleached all-purpose flour
- ½ teaspoon fine sea salt
- 1 (.25-ounce) package active dry yeast
- 2 cups water, warmed to 95 degrees
- 6 tablespoons extra-virgin olive oil, divided, plus more for pans

**TOPPING**

- 1 tablespoon olive oil, plus more for brushing
- 1 apple (Sweet Sixteen; see head note), cored and chopped
- 8 ounces cremini mushrooms, sliced thin
- 1 cup sliced red onion

sea salt and freshly ground black pepper

1 tablespoon cornmeal

1 tablespoon minced fresh rosemary

2 tablespoons pine nuts

4 ounces goat cheese (Stickney Hill), crumbled

..........................

Preheat oven to 425 degrees. For the dough, use a stand mixer fitted with the dough hook attachment to mix the flour and salt. In a glass measuring cup, mix together the yeast and water, making sure the water is not too hot or it will kill the yeast. Let sit for 2 minutes to let the yeast activate. With the mixer running on low, slowly pour in the water and yeast and 4 tablespoons olive oil. Mix on medium speed for 5 minutes, until dough comes together. Drizzle another tablespoon of olive oil over the dough, and turn over the dough to coat. Cover with a tea towel or plastic wrap and set in a warm place to rise for 1½ hours.

Meanwhile, prepare the topping. In a large bowl, toss 1 tablespoon olive oil with the apple, mushrooms, and onions. Line a rimmed baking sheet with parchment paper and spread apple mixture on it. Sprinkle with sea salt and black pepper. Roast for 15 minutes. Remove from oven and set aside.

After the dough has risen, uncover, punch down, and divide in two. Shape each half into a ball, then let rest for 5 minutes. On a lightly floured work surface, roll out dough to a 10-inch circle. Brush 2 (10-inch) cake pans with olive oil and sprinkle the bottoms with cornmeal. Place dough rounds into prepared pans. Cover and let rise for 30 minutes. Poke dough down with your fingertips. Brush with olive oil. Scatter the apple mixture on the prepared focaccia dough, followed by the rosemary, pine nuts, and goat cheese. Drizzle with remaining tablespoon olive oil. Let rest for 15 minutes.

Bake for 20 to 25 minutes, until golden brown. Cut each focaccia into 6 wedges. Garnish with crushed flaked sea salt and freshly ground black pepper. ◇

## CARAMELIZED RED ONION, ROASTED APPLE, AND KALE PIZZA

*Make Friday night pizza night. Apples of any variety lend a nice complexity to the earthy flavors of Lacinato kale and squash.* **SERVES 6**

......................................

1 large red onion, sliced

2 apples, cored and chopped

4 cups chopped Lacinato kale

2 cups chopped butternut squash

¼ cup olive oil

¼ cup balsamic vinegar (Locust Lane)

¼ teaspoon sea salt

¼ teaspoon freshly ground black pepper

2 fresh whole-wheat pizza doughs (recipe follows)

2 tablespoons cornmeal

2 (4-ounce) mozzarella balls (BelGioioso), chopped

......................................

Preheat oven to 425 degrees. In a large bowl, mix together the onions, apples, kale, and squash. Drizzle with olive oil and balsamic vinegar, and spread mixture onto 2 rimmed baking sheets. Sprinkle with salt and pepper. Roast for 15 minutes, then stir and continue to roast for another 15 minutes. Remove from the oven and increase heat to 450 degrees.

While the apple mixture is roasting, prepare the dough. On a floured surface, roll out each dough to a 12-inch circle. Sprinkle cornmeal onto a pizza peel. Place one dough on the peel and spread with half the apple mixture. Dot with half the mozzarella. Bake for about 14 minutes, until crust is browned and cheese melts. Repeat with remaining ingredients.

*Tip:* If you are making 1 pizza, save the remaining roasted apple mixture for another use. It is delicious as a side dish or mixed with pasta. ◊

# Pizza Dough

*Many people tell me they are afraid of working with yeast, but once you get your fingers into this dough you will realize why it's so fun to make pizza from scratch. The bonus of making your own dough is the amazing flavor.*

**MAKES ENOUGH FOR 2 (12-INCH) PIZZAS**

- ¾ cup water, warmed to 95–105 degrees
- 2 teaspoons sugar
- 1½ teaspoons active dry yeast
- 3 tablespoons extra-virgin olive oil, divided
- 1 teaspoon kosher salt
- 1¾ cups unbleached all-purpose flour, divided
- ¾ cup whole wheat flour
- 1 tablespoon cornmeal

In a medium bowl, mix together water, sugar, and yeast. Let stand for about 5 minutes. Stir in 2 tablespoons olive oil and salt. Mix in 1¼ cups all-purpose flour and all the whole wheat flour until combined. Turn dough out onto a lightly floured work surface. Knead for about 5 minutes, adding up to ½ cup remaining flour as needed. The dough should be smooth and slightly sticky. Place dough in a large bowl and top with remaining table-spoon olive oil. Turn to coat with oil. Cover the bowl with plastic wrap and allow dough to double for about 1½ hours.

Preheat oven to 425 degrees. When the dough has doubled, divide in half. On a floured work surface, roll out one dough to 12 inches round. Sprinkle a pizza peel with cornmeal. Place one dough round on the peel. Top as desired and bake as directed. Repeat with other dough. ◇

## Kale–La Crescent Apple Wild Mushroom Ravioli

*The La Crescent apple, available in late August through early September, is juicy, sweet, and tart. I love pairing this dish with another Minnesota original: Sovereign Estate's wine made with La Crescent grapes.* **SERVES 4**

- 2 tablespoons olive oil
- 1 cup sliced sweet onion
- 4 ounces thin-sliced salami, cut into slivers
- 5 ounces shiitake mushrooms, sliced
- 2 cloves garlic, minced
- 2 medium apples (La Crescent), cored and chopped
- ½ cup La Crescent wine or Riesling, or substitute apple cider or hard apple cider
- ½ bunch kale, chopped (4 cups)
- sea salt and freshly ground black pepper
- pinch red pepper flakes
- 1 (9-ounce) package cheese and mushroom ravioli (Three Bridges), cooked and drained
- ¼ cup pine nuts, toasted
- 4 ounces Parmesan (SarVecchio), shaved

Set a large skillet over medium-high heat, and add the olive oil, onions, and salami. Cook, stirring, until the onions are soft, about 5 minutes. Add the mushrooms, garlic, and apples, and continue to cook for another 5 minutes. When the apples are beginning to soften, add the wine. Stir in the kale, ½ teaspoon sea salt, ¼ teaspoon black pepper, and red pepper flakes. Reduce heat and cover. Cook for about 10 more minutes, until the kale is wilted.

Toss drained ravioi with the apple-kale mixture. Divide among 4 warm pasta bowls, and garnish with pine nuts and shaved Parmesan. ◊

## Spaghetti with Tomato-Apple Sauce

*This recipe, inspired by author and TV chef Lidia Bastianich, hails from Northern Italy, where many apples are grown. In fact, Italy ranks fourth in the world for apple production. Italians long ago discovered the genius of adding apples to many dishes to create complex flavors. Most varieties work well in this recipe; I use Honeycrisp or McIntosh.* **SERVES 6–8**

............................

16  ounces spaghetti

¼  cup extra-virgin olive oil

 2  large apples, cored and chopped

 1  medium onion, chopped

 3  ribs celery, chopped

 2  cloves garlic, minced

½  cup apple cider

 1  (15.5-ounce) can diced tomatoes

 1  teaspoon sea salt

½  teaspoon freshly ground black pepper

    pinch crushed red pepper flakes

 1  cup freshly grated Parmesan

1¼  cups chopped Italian parsley

............................

Fill a large pot with water, set over high heat, and bring to a boil. Cook the spaghetti al dente according to package directions. Drain and keep warm.

Meanwhile, set a large skillet over medium-high heat and add the olive oil. When the oil is shimmering, add the apples, onions, and celery, and cook, stirring occasionally, for about 10 minutes. Stir in the garlic. Pour in the cider and cook to reduce the liquid, scraping the bottom of the pan to loosen any browned bits. When the liquid has been absorbed, stir in the tomatoes and heat through. Season with salt, black pepper, and red pepper flakes. Toss the sauce with the spaghetti and serve in a warmed bowl. Garnish with Parmesan and parsley.  ◇

## Rainbow Trout with Apple Gremolata

*Gremolata, a classic condiment usually served with osso buco (braised veal shank) and traditionally made with parsley, lemon zest, and garlic, offers bright flavors to complement a silky, rich entrée. This rendition plays with that contrast and with the addition of sweet apples like McIntosh. The presentation of a whole trout is exquisite, and the taste is sumptuous.* **SERVES 4**

1 cup panko bread crumbs

½ cup minced Italian parsley

zest and juice of 1 lemon

2 cloves garlic, minced

sea salt

4 tablespoons canola oil, divided

2 shallots, minced

2 apples, peeled, cored, and cut into half-inch pieces

2 cups Fresh Apple Cider (page 160)

4 (12-ounce) whole rainbow trout, rinsed and patted dry

freshly ground black pepper

¼ cup apple brandy

¼ cup heavy cream

2 tablespoons butter, cut into pieces

In a small skillet set over medium-high heat, toast the bread crumbs until golden. Remove from heat. In a medium bowl, mix together the parsley, lemon zest, garlic, and ½ teaspoon sea salt. Stir in the toasted bread crumbs and set aside.

In a large skillet set over medium heat, warm 2 tablespoons oil. Add the shallots and cook, stirring occasionally, until fragrant and translucent, about 4 minutes. Increase heat to medium high and stir in the apples and lemon juice. Cook, stirring occasionally, for about 8 minutes. Stir in the apple cider. Continue to cook until liquid is thickened and reduced by half.

While the sauce is simmering, prepare the trout. Season on both sides with salt and pepper. Set a large skillet over medium-high heat and warm remaining 2 tablespoons oil. Place the trout in the skillet, alternating head and tail to fit. Cook for about 6 minutes, then flip and cook for an additional 6 minutes, until cooked through. Carefully remove fish from pan and set on a platter. After a few minutes, remove the bones (if the fishmonger did not do so). Tent with foil to keep warm.

To finish the sauce, reduce heat to medium and stir in the apple brandy. Then stir in the cream and butter. Stir in ¼ teaspoon sea salt and ⅛ teaspoon black pepper and remove from heat.

Lay one trout open on each of 4 dinner plates. Spoon 2 tablespoons gremolata in the center of each fish. Gently fold trout back together. Spoon sauce evenly over each trout. Sprinkle with bread crumb mixture. ◊

## Seared Scallops with Apple Pancetta Chutney

*Rich, sweet, glorious scallops are complemented perfectly with a lively apple pancetta chutney. The sum of the parts creates a symphony of flavors. Choose a sweet-tart apple such as Zestar, Cortland, or SnowSweet.* **SERVES 4**

- 2 tablespoons olive oil, divided
- ½ cup minced sweet onion
- 4 ounces pancetta (see tip), diced
- 1 tablespoon fresh thyme leaves
- ¼ teaspoon sea salt
- ¼ teaspoon freshly ground black pepper
- ¼ cup Fresh Apple Cider (page 160)
- 2 medium apples, cored and diced
- 12 Alaskan or sea scallops (see tip), patted dry
- 2 tablespoons butter

Set a large skillet over medium-high heat and add 1 tablespoon olive oil. Stir in the onion, pancetta, thyme, salt, and pepper, and cook until the onions are translucent and the pancetta is crispy, about 6 minutes. Add the apple cider and apples. Simmer until the apples are soft and the liquid is reduced, about 15 minutes. Transfer chutney to a small saucepan and keep warm on low heat.

Wipe out skillet and set over high heat. Add remaining tablespoon olive oil. When the oil is just beginning to shimmer, add the scallops, being careful not to crowd the pan. Wait to move the scallops until the bottoms are golden brown, about 3 minutes. Then flip the scallops and add the butter. Cook for another 3 minutes. As butter melts, spoon it over the scallops. Divide the chutney among 4 plates and arrange scallops on top.

*Tips:* La Quercia in Norwalk, Iowa, and Red Table Meat Company in Minneapolis, Minnesota, produce excellent pancetta. Alaskan scallops are responsibly harvested. ◇

# Braised Pork with Roasted Onions and Apples

*Pork and apples: the quintessential combination. Germany, Italy, and France all have their take on this classic. Choose a firm apple that will hold its texture as it cooks.* **SERVES 6–8**

sea salt and freshly ground black pepper

1 tablespoon minced fresh rosemary

1 (3-pound) pork shoulder roast

2 tablespoons olive oil

4 cups apple cider

4 apples, cored and sliced into wedges

3 onions, sliced

1 pound dried cannellini beans, soaked overnight and drained

2 whole cloves

4 juniper berries

1 bay leaf

½ cup apple brandy

Preheat oven to 300 degrees. In a small bowl, stir together 2 teaspoons salt, 2 teaspoons black pepper, and rosemary. Rub spices over roast. In a Dutch oven set over medium-high heat, warm olive oil. Add roast to the pan, searing one side for about 4 minutes, then rotating and repeating until seared on all sides. Reduce heat. Add cider, apples, onions, beans, cloves, juniper berries, and bay leaf. Cover and braise in oven for approximately 2½ hours. Remove roast, apples, and onions to a platter and cover with aluminum foil. Set pan over medium-high heat, add brandy to cooking liquid, and simmer until thickened, about 15 minutes. Taste and adjust seasoning. Spoon sauce over roast.  ◊

## Pork Chops with Apples, Onions, and Herbs de Provence

*Although most of the apples grown in France come from the northern region of Normandy, this dish offers a little southern French spin. Choose any fresh apple from the orchard or market, perhaps a sweet one like SweeTango, Red Baron, or Honeygold, and serve with a grain side.* **SERVES 2 GENEROUSLY OR 4 AS PART OF A LARGER MEAL**

............................

1 tablespoon soy sauce

1 clove garlic, minced

2 (8-ounce) center-cut boneless pork chops

1 tablespoon olive oil

1 medium sweet white onion, sliced

2 medium sweet apples (see head note), cored and chopped

4 ounces chanterelle mushrooms

1 teaspoon herbs de Provence (see tip)

pinch kosher salt

¼ cup hard cider

juice of 1 lemon

1 tablespoon butter

............................

In a glass container, stir together the soy sauce and garlic and add the pork chops, turning to coat. Marinate in the refrigerator for at least 1 hour; discard marinade. Set a large skillet over medium-high heat and add the olive oil. When the oil is shimmering, sear the pork chops for 4 to 5 minutes on one side and then flip to sear the other side. Reduce heat to medium. Add the onions, apples, mushrooms, herbs, and salt. Cook the pork chops until internal temperature registers 140 degrees on a meat thermometer. Remove the chops to a platter and cover with aluminum foil. Continue to cook the apple mixture until tender, about 10 more minutes. Pour in cider and cook to reduce the liquid, scraping the bottom of the pan to loosen any browned bits. When the liquid is absorbed, swirl in the lemon juice and butter. Taste and adjust seasonings if necessary. Serve apple mixture with the pork.

*Tip:* Herbs de Provence is a blend of dried rosemary, marjoram, basil, tarragon, green peppercorns, lavender buds, and fennel. The Golden Fig's version is my favorite: goldenfig.com. If you can't find herbs de Provence, substitute Italian seasoning. ◊

# Apple, Mushroom, and Pancetta Risotto

*Earthy flavors mingle in this classic Italian dish. A firm, tart apple works best.* **SERVES 6**

...........................

1 ounce dried porcini

4 ounces pancetta, sliced

1 tablespoon extra-virgin olive oil

6 tablespoons (¾ stick) butter, divided

8 ounces cremini mushrooms, sliced thin

1 tablespoon minced fresh thyme

pinch sea salt

pinch freshly ground black pepper

1 cup sparkling hard cider, divided

5 cups chicken broth

2 shallots, minced

1 apple, cored and minced

2 cups arborio rice

¾ cup freshly grated Parmesan

...........................

In a small bowl, combine 1 cup hot water and dried porcini. Set aside to reconstitute. Set a large skillet over medium-high heat and fry the pancetta until crispy. Remove and drain on a paper towel. When cool enough to handle, coarsely chop and set aside. Add the olive oil and 1 tablespoon butter to the pan. Add the cremini mushrooms, season with thyme, salt, and pepper, and cook, stirring, until browned. Chop the reconstituted porcini and add to the pan with the soaking liquid and ¼ cup cider. Cook to reduce the liquid, scraping the bottom of the pan to loosen any browned bits. Remove from heat, cover, and set aside.

In a large saucepan set over medium heat, warm the chicken broth. Set a Dutch oven over medium heat and melt 2 tablespoons butter. When it is beginning to sizzle, stir in the shallots, apples, and rice. Cook, stirring, for about 4 minutes. When the rice begins to brown, add ½ cup cider. Continue to cook, stirring, until cider is absorbed. Then stir in 1 cup chicken broth. Continue to cook, stirring, until broth is absorbed. Add the remaining ¼ cup cider, stirring until absorbed. Keep adding broth, 1 cup at a time, stirring constantly, until all of the broth is used and rice is tender but not mushy. Stir in remaining 3 tablespoons butter and Parmesan. Fold in the mushrooms. Garnish with chopped pancetta. ◊

## Porchetta with Roasted Apples and Roots

*This recipe combines apples and root vegetables for an irresistible version of a traditional comfort food,* porchetta, *or Italian pork roast—a staple for fall Sunday dinners. Choose a firm, tart apple, and serve with polenta, steamed kale, and apple wine.* **SERVES 8–10**

...........................

2  tablespoons fennel seeds, toasted

1  tablespoon coarse sea salt

2  teaspoons black peppercorns

1  teaspoon crushed red pepper flakes

1  tablespoon minced fresh sage

1  teaspoon minced fresh rosemary

1  (3-pound) pork shoulder roast

3  tablespoons olive oil

8  cloves garlic, minced

4  apples, cored and chopped

1  large onion, chopped

2 parsnips, peeled and sliced

2 carrots, peeled and sliced

1 red garnet yam or sweet potato, peeled and chopped

1 cup apple wine (Chankaska Creek), or substitute white wine

½ cup vegetable broth or Apple Tisane (page 159) or apple cider

..........................

Preheat oven to 325 degrees. In a small bowl, mix together fennel seeds, sea salt, peppercorns, red pepper flakes, sage, and rosemary. Rub spice mixture over roast. Set a Dutch oven over medium-high heat and warm the olive oil. Add roast to the pan, searing one side for about 4 minutes, then rotating and repeating until seared on all sides. Cover and place in the oven, roasting for approximately 2 hours, until internal temperature registers 145 degrees on a meat thermometer. Add the garlic, apples, onions, parsnips, carrots, and yams. Increase oven temperature to 400 degrees and roast for 30 minutes. Remove the pork, apples, and vegetables to a platter and cover to keep warm. Set the Dutch oven over medium heat and pour in the apple wine. Cook to reduce the liquid, scraping the bottom of the pan to loosen any browned bits. Add the broth or cider and cook, stirring occasionally, until reduced by half. Slice the pork and pour pan sauce over roast, apples, and vegetables.  ◇

## Southwestern Chicken Sausage with Apples and Sweet Corn

*This recipe is easy to cut in half for a small batch or double for a potluck. I recommend a tart apple like Regent, Cortland, or Honeycrisp.* **SERVES 4**

.........................

1 cup farro

2 ears fresh sweet corn

2 tablespoons olive oil

1 medium onion, sliced

3 cups chopped tart apples (see head note)

1 cup chopped red bell pepper

1 poblano chile, seeded and chopped

1 (12-ounce) package precooked chicken sausages (Bilinski), sliced

1 clove garlic, minced

½ teaspoon smoked paprika

1 teaspoon ground chipotle pepper

salt and freshly ground black pepper

½ cup crumbled Cotija, or substitute feta

¾ cup chopped cilantro

.........................

In a medium saucepan, bring 2 cups water to a boil. Add the farro, cover, and reduce heat to simmer. Cook for 25 to 30 minutes.

Meanwhile, use a sharp knife to remove the kernels from the corn. Set a large skillet over medium-high heat and add olive oil. Add the kernels, onions, apples, red pepper, and poblano and cook, stirring, for about 8 minutes. Add the sausage and garlic, stirring to combine. Sprinkle with paprika, chipotle pepper, salt, and pepper. Reduce heat to low and cover. Cook for about 15 more minutes, until heated through and tender.

To serve, divide farro among 4 bowls. Spoon sausage-apple mixture on top, and garnish with a sprinkle of Cotija and cilantro. ◊

# GINGER CURRY APPLE TURKEY BAKE

*This easy weeknight meal solution, a great combination of flavors, was inspired by my daughter, Marissa.* **SERVES 6**

- 2 cups low-sodium chicken stock
- 1 cup brown jasmine rice
- sea salt
- 1 tablespoon minced fresh ginger
- 1 tablespoon curry powder
- 3 medium apples (Paula Red), cored and chopped
- 2 ribs celery, sliced
- ½ large onion, chopped
- ½ cup sliced red bell pepper
- 2 tablespoons olive oil
- 1 rotisserie turkey breast
- freshly ground black pepper

Preheat oven to 400 degrees. In a medium saucepan, bring chicken stock to a boil. Stir in rice and ¼ teaspoon sea salt, reduce heat to simmer, cover, and cook for about 45 minutes, until liquid is absorbed and rice is tender.

In a large bowl, mix together the ginger, curry powder, apples, celery, onions, red pepper, and olive oil. Place the turkey breast on a rimmed baking sheet and spread the apple mixture around the turkey. Roast for about 25 minutes, until the mixture is golden brown and tender. Taste and add salt and black pepper if needed. Serve with rice. ◊

## Apple and Grain Thai Bowl

*An assortment of elements put together in a shallow bowl can make for a healthy everyday meal. Call it a crossover cuisine: it can be for breakfast, lunch, or dinner; switch up the seasonings and it can be Asian, Latin, Mediterranean, or Moroccan. It's kind of a stir-fry, but if you add more broth it's kind of a soup. It's nutritious and delicious: a winning combination.* **SERVES 4**

- 4 cups chicken stock, divided
- 1 cup quinoa, barley, or farro
- 1 tablespoon extra-virgin olive oil
- 4 skinless, boneless chicken thighs, chopped
- 1 cup chopped onion
- 2 cups chopped apple
- 1 cup minced yam
- 1 teaspoon minced fresh ginger
- 1 clove garlic, minced
- 1 fresh Thai red pepper, seeded and minced
- 1 tablespoon fish sauce
- 2 teaspoons red curry paste
- 2 teaspoons Thai seasoning (Thai Garden; see tip)
- pinch sea salt
- 1 cup tightly packed chopped kale
- ¾ cup chopped Thai basil or cilantro

In a large saucepan, bring 3 cups chicken stock to a boil. Stir in grain, reduce heat to a simmer, cover, and cook until tender: about 15 minutes for quinoa and 35 minutes for barley or farro.

Meanwhile, set a large skillet over medium-high heat. Add olive oil and chicken and cook, stirring, for about 6 minutes, until cooked through. Add the onions, apples, yams, ginger, garlic, Thai red pepper, fish sauce, curry paste, seasoning, and salt. Cook, stirring, for about 8 minutes, until the onions are tender and translucent and the mixture begins to brown. Stir in the kale and remaining cup chicken stock. Cook until kale is wilted. Divide the grain among 4 warm, shallow bowls. Scoop the chicken mixture on top. Garnish with Thai basil.

*Tip:* For Thai seasoning blend, substitute ¼ teaspoon each of cumin, coriander, nutmeg, cinnamon, cardamom, and cloves. ✧

## CHEDDAR CIDER FONDUE

*Apples and Cheddar—a match made in heaven. The key to the success of this fondue is to pick a really good-quality cheese and match with a really good apple. SnowSweet and Honeycrisp are great choices because they are less likely to brown.* **SERVES 8**

- 24 ounces sharp Cheddar, shredded
- 8 ounces extra-sharp Cheddar, shredded
- 2 tablespoons cornstarch
- 1 clove garlic, halved
- 1 cup hard cider
- 1 tablespoon Calvados or apple brandy
- ⅛ teaspoon cayenne
- pinch sea salt
- 2 apples, cored and sliced in wedges
- 1 loaf artisanal bread, cut into bite-size pieces

In a large bowl, stir together the cheeses and cornstarch. Rub the garlic over the inside of a fondue pot or other heavy-bottomed pot; discard garlic. Set pot over medium heat. Add the hard cider and heat for a few minutes. Slowly add the cheese, a cup at a time, stirring constantly, until it is all incorporated and smooth. Stir in Calvados, cayenne, and salt. Dip apples and bread in the fondue. ◊

# SWEETS

The aroma of an apple dessert baking in the oven: an amazing sensory memory that spans generations and cultures. Apples' ambrosial quality provides a heavenly punctuation mark for any feast. From a rustic crostada to an ethereal apple custard cake, the options are as endless as the number of cultivars. Apples are usually peeled for desserts; however, at times leaving the peel on adds to the visual charm and, always, the nutritional value. Along with flavor, consider texture when choosing apples for baking. Some will bake down to a very saucy consistency, while others will remain chunky and toothsome.

## APPLE ALMOND BISCOTTI

*Biscotti are Italian biscuits (cookies) that are twice baked, best enjoyed with a dessert wine like Vin Santo. Try dunking this Minnesota version in hot spiced apple cider, warmed apple brandy, or one of the region's dessert wines.* **MAKES 24 COOKIES**

- 1 cup sugar
- 8 tablespoons (1 stick) unsalted butter, melted
- 3 tablespoons Amaretto
- 2 teaspoons almond extract
- 1 teaspoon vanilla
- 1 cup sliced almonds
- ½ cup chopped dried apples (page 24)
- 3 large eggs, lightly beaten
- 2¾ cups unbleached all-purpose flour
- 1½ teaspoons baking powder
- ¼ teaspoon salt

In a large bowl, stir together sugar, butter, Amaretto, almond extract, and vanilla. Stir in almonds, apples, and eggs, mixing well. Stir in flour, baking powder, and salt until just combined. Cover bowl and refrigerate dough for 30 minutes.

Preheat oven to 350 degrees and set a rack in the middle position. Using moistened hands, halve dough and form 2 (10x4–inch) loaves on an ungreased baking sheet. Bake until pale golden, about 30 minutes. Carefully transfer loaves to a rack and let cool for 15 minutes.

Use a serrated knife to cut loaves into ¾–inch slices. Arrange biscotti on a clean baking sheet and bake until golden, 20 to 25 minutes. Transfer to a rack and cool completely. Biscotti improve in flavor if made 1 to 2 days ahead. Store in an airtight container at room temperature.  ◊

# HONEY-APPLE CRÈME BRÛLÉE /
# MIELE E MELA CRÈME BRÛLÉE
....................................................

*This dessert is a little fussy but oh so worth it—a real crowd pleaser. Given all the steps, it's best to prepare a day or two ahead. Honeycrisp is beautiful in this recipe, or choose another firm, sweet-tart apple like a Cortland or Regent.* **SERVES 12**

..............................

### FOR THE APPLES

6 medium apples (see head note), peeled, cored, and chopped

4 tablespoons (½ stick) butter

2 tablespoon raw or Demerara or natural cane sugar

..............................

Set a large skillet over medium heat and add the apples, butter, and sugar. Cook, stirring, until apples begin to soften and turn a golden brown, about 15 minutes. Set aside.

### FOR THE CARAMEL SAUCE

1½ cups honey

½ cup heavy cream

1 tablespoon butter

1 teaspoon vanilla

⅛ teaspoon salt

..............................

In a heavy saucepan, stir together the honey and cream. Set over medium-high heat, bring to a boil, and cook until the mixture registers 238 degrees on a candy thermometer, approximately 15 minutes. Remove from heat and stir in the butter, vanilla, and salt. Set aside to cool.

**FOR THE CRÈME**

3  cups heavy cream

1  cup whole milk

1  vanilla bean, split and scraped

1  cup raw or Demerara or natural cane sugar, divided

6  large egg yolks

..............................

Preheat oven to 325 degrees. In a heavy saucepan, stir together the cream, milk, and vanilla bean and seeds. Set over medium-high heat and bring to a boil. When mixture begins to boil, remove from heat. Cover and let steep for 15 minutes. Remove and discard vanilla bean.

In a medium bowl, whisk together ½ cup sugar and the egg yolks until the color begins to lighten. Add the warm cream, ½ cup at a time, whisking to blend.

Place 12 (8-ounce) ramekins in a cake pan. Divide the apples among the ramekins, approximately ¼ cup each. Divide caramel sauce among the ramekins, about 2 tablespoons each. Carefully pour in the cream mixture, filling each ramekin almost to the top. Add hot water to the cake pan, filling until the water is halfway up the ramekins. Bake for approximately 40 minutes, until center is nearly set. Remove ramekins from the pan, cool to room temperature, and refrigerate for at least 2 hours or up to 3 days.

To serve, bring to room temperature. Sprinkle ramekins evenly with remaining ½ cup sugar. Use a small, handheld kitchen torch to melt the sugar, or place ramekins under broiler for a few minutes. Let sit for at least 5 minutes before serving. ◊

## APPLE PANNA COTTA

Panna cotta, *literally "cooked cream," is traditional comfort food that most likely originated in the Piedmont region of northern Italy, where cream and honey are abundant. Today it's found on the dessert trays of many restaurants that employ innovative presentations and ingredients. For a textured sauce, choose a firm apple like Haralson or Ginger Gold.* **SERVES 8**

3 medium apples (see head note), cored and chopped

1 cup apple cider

1 teaspoon Apple Spice Blend (page 15)

2 tablespoons apple brandy

2 teaspoons vanilla, divided

2 cups (1 pint) heavy cream (organic preferred), divided

1 package (2½ teaspoons) unflavored gelatin

¼ cup honey

1 cup buttermilk

½ cup hazelnuts, toasted, skins removed, coarsely chopped (see tip)

In a saucepan set over medium heat, combine the apples, cider, and spice blend and cook, stirring occasionally, for about 15 minutes. The apples will soften and a syrupy sauce will begin to form. Stir in the brandy and continue to cook for about 2 minutes. Remove from heat, stir in 1 teaspoon vanilla, and set aside.

In a small bowl, mix ½ cup heavy cream with gelatin, stirring to combine. Set aside until gelatin softens, about 10 minutes.

In a medium saucepan, combine remaining 1½ cups heavy cream and honey; bring to a boil and then remove from heat. Whisk in gelatin mixture until gelatin dissolves, about 2 minutes. Add buttermilk and remaining teaspoon vanilla, whisking to combine. Divide mixture equally among 8 (8-ounce) dessert bowls. Refrigerate, uncovered, for at least 1 hour or overnight.

To serve, spoon desired amount of apples over panna cotta and garnish with hazelnuts.

*Tips:* Toast hazelnuts in a single layer on a baking sheet in a 275-degree oven for 15 to 20 minutes. Remove from oven, wrap nuts in a tea towel, and when cool rub to remove skins.

For traditional molded panna cotta, lightly grease 8 (4-ounce) ramekins. Divide panna cotta equally among ramekins. Chill as directed. To unmold, loosen panna cotta by running a small knife around the edge. If necessary, dip bottom of ramekin in hot water bath for a few seconds, then invert onto plates. Spoon sauce over top and sprinkle with hazelnuts.  ◇

# Apple Crostada with Salted Caramel Sauce

*This rustic free-form tart is made with a short crust pastry dough. The best thing about rustic desserts is that they are never too fancy but always a special treat. If the edges of the dough are irregular, it's all the more charming. Pick a sweet apple. If it has a thick peel, remove it; otherwise, leave it on for extra color and a homespun feel.* **SERVES 6**

### PASTRY

1 cup unbleached all-purpose flour

1 tablespoon granulated sugar

pinch salt

6 tablespoons (¾ stick) cold unsalted butter, cut into pieces

1 large egg yolk

### SALTED CARAMEL SAUCE

4 tablespoons (½ stick) unsalted butter

½ cup heavy cream

1 cup packed brown sugar

2 teaspoons vanilla

pinch salt

### FILLING

3 apples, cored and sliced thin

2 tablespoons turbinado or light brown sugar, divided

1 teaspoon Apple Spice Blend (page 15)

1 large egg, lightly beaten

½ teaspoon flaked sea salt

Line a baking sheet with parchment paper and set aside. For the crust, in a medium bowl, whisk together the flour, granulated sugar, and salt. Use your fingers or a pastry blender to mix the butter into the flour. When the mixture resembles coarse meal, add the egg and stir until the dough forms a ball. Wrap in plastic and let rest in the refrigerator for about 1 hour.

To make the caramel sauce, in a small saucepan set over medium heat, combine the butter, cream, and brown sugar. Bring to a simmer and stir until the sugar is dissolved. Continue to cook, stirring occasionally, for about 10 minutes, until sauce is smooth. Remove from heat and stir in the vanilla and salt. Keep warm.

Preheat oven to 375 degrees. In a large bowl, combine the apples, 1 tablespoon turbinado sugar, and spice blend, tossing well to coat. Set aside.

On a lightly floured work surface, roll out the dough into a thin 12-inch circle. Transfer to prepared baking sheet. Arrange the apples on the dough, leaving a 2-inch border. Fold the dough edges over the apples. Brush the dough with the beaten egg. Sprinkle the crostata with the remaining tablespoon turbinado sugar. Bake for about 25 minutes, until golden brown and bubbling. Serve with a generous drizzle of caramel sauce and a sprinkle of flaked sea salt. ◈

## Individual Haralson Tartes Tatin

*Tarte tatin is an upside-down caramelized apple tart, said to be the accidental invention of Stéphanie Tatin of the Hotel Tatin, in Lamotte-Beuvron, France. The idea is to bake the crust on top and then invert it for serving. This variation is quick to make, especially if you use store-bought pie crust.*

**SERVES 8**

........................

1 cup apple cider

¾ cup granulated sugar

2 tablespoons butter

2 tablespoons spiced or dark rum

4 apples (Haralson), peeled, cored, and cut into eighths

3 tablespoons raw or Demerara or natural cane sugar, divided

pastry for 2-crust pie

1 quart vanilla bean ice cream

........................

Preheat oven to 400 degrees. Place 8 (8-ounce) ramekins on a rimmed baking sheet. In a medium heavy-bottomed saucepan set over medium heat, stir together the cider and granulated sugar and cook until the mixture begins to caramelize, about 15 minutes. It should look more syrupy than watery and should leave a track when you run your finger over the back of your stirring spoon. Remove from heat and stir in the butter and rum. Spoon 2 tablespoons of the caramel sauce into each ramekin. Add 4 apple slices to each ramekin and sprinkle with a teaspoon of Demerara sugar. Roll out pie dough and cut circles to cover each ramekin. Lay the dough on top and fold in the edges. Pierce the top with a knife to make one hole in the middle and three around the sides.

Bake for about 35 minutes, until golden brown. Remove from oven and let cool for at least 15 minutes. To serve, invert each ramekin onto a dessert plate and top with a scoop of ice cream. Sprinkle with Demerara sugar. ◊

## Puff Pastry Honey-Glazed Apple Tarts

*If you're short on time but want to impress your guests, make this your go-to recipe. Puff pastry never fails to kick your dessert up a notch. Haralson apples, with their sweet-tart taste, are an excellent choice for this tart.* MAKES 4 (5-INCH) TARTS

- 1 sheet frozen puff pastry dough, thawed but still cool
- 2 medium apples (see head note), peeled, cored, and sliced thin
- 2 tablespoons raw sugar (organic preferred; can substitute Demerara or turbinado), divided
- 3 tablespoons butter, melted
- 2 tablespoons honey
- ½ teaspoon almond extract
- 1 cup (8 ounces) mascarpone
- 2 tablespoons almonds, toasted

Preheat oven to 400 degrees. Line a baking sheet with parchment paper and set aside. Roll out the dough to a 12x12–inch square and cut into 4 (5-inch) rounds. Place rounds on prepared baking sheet; discard scraps. Arrange the apples on the dough rounds by overlapping in a circle. Make a large circle first, leaving about a quarter-inch edge, then overlap 5 more slices in each center. Sprinkle apples with 1 tablespoon sugar and drizzle with butter. Allow the tarts to rest for about 10 minutes before baking. Bake for about 25 minutes, until golden brown. Remove from the oven and drizzle with honey. In a small bowl, whisk the almond extract and remaining tablespoon sugar into the mascarpone. Serve the tarts with a dollop of mascarpone and a sprinkle of almonds.

*Tip:* To make 1 large tart to serve 6, cut dough into a 12-inch round and proceed with the recipe. ◇

## Rustic Umbrian Apple Roll / Le Rocciata

*Many cultures serve a thin pastry dessert filled with layers of chopped apples. In Italy, you can find this popular dish in the fall when fresh apples and walnuts appear in the markets of the central region of Umbria. The curious name translates to "the rock," in reference to the landscape. Choose a sweet apple for this cousin of the apple strudel.* **SERVES 8**

¼ cup extra-virgin olive oil

2 tablespoons hard or regular cider

2 large egg yolks

2½ cups unbleached all-purpose flour

¼ cup sugar, plus more for sprinkling

pinch salt

6 tablespoons (¾ stick) cold butter, cut into pieces, plus 1 tablespoon, melted

2 apples, peeled, cored, and minced

1 cup walnuts

⅓ cup honey

½ cup golden raisins

1 teaspoon Apple Spice Blend (page 15)

2 tablespoons apple brandy

In a glass measuring cup, stir together olive oil, cider, and egg yolks. Set aside. In a large bowl, whisk together the flour, ¼ cup sugar, and salt. Add the diced butter and mix in with a pastry blender until it resembles coarse meal. Use a wooden spoon to stir in the oil-egg mixture until all the flour is incorporated. Turn out onto a floured work surface and knead for a few minutes. Divide into 4 pieces. Wrap in plastic and refrigerate for 1 hour.

Preheat oven to 350 degrees. In a large bowl, toss the apples, nuts, honey, raisins, spice blend, and brandy. Roll each piece of dough between 2 sheets of parchment to form 4 (12x8–inch) rectangles. Wrap and refrigerate for 20 minutes.

Working with one rectangle at a time, lay prepared dough on a floured surface. Spoon 1 cup apple mixture down the middle. Roll up the pastry the long way and press to seal. Place on baking sheet sealed-side down. Brush with melted butter. Sprinkle with sugar. Repeat with remaining ingredients. Bake for 35 to 40 minutes, until golden brown.  ◊

## APPLE CRUMBLE

*Rustic and homey, a crumble is similar to a crisp. With fruit on the bottom and a buttery crispy crumble topping, it's a plentiful dessert for family events or potlucks. Crumbles can be made ahead and frozen. When you are ready to serve, rewarm in the oven and serve with a scoop of vanilla ice cream. This recipe is updated with the addition of whole wheat flour and ground flax.* **SERVES 16**

1½  cups raw or natural cane or Demerara sugar, divided
2½  cups old-fashioned oats
⅓  cup whole wheat flour
⅔  cup unbleached all-purpose flour
¼  cup ground flaxseed
1  cup (2 sticks) unsalted butter, cut into half-inch cubes
4  pounds tart apples, peeled, cored, each cut into 12 slices
   juice of 1 lemon
1  teaspoon cinnamon
½  cup chopped pecans
1  quart vanilla ice cream

Preheat oven to 375 degrees. Grease a 9x13–inch baking dish. In a large bowl, stir together 1 cup sugar, oats, flours, and flaxseed. Add butter and mix into the flour with your fingertips. In another bowl, toss the apples with lemon juice, cinnamon, and remaining ½ cup sugar. Transfer apple mixture to the baking dish and scoop flour mixture on top. Bake for about 50 minutes, until the apples are bubbling and the topping is golden brown. Sprinkle with pecans and return to the oven for 5 more minutes. Spoon warm crumble into bowls and serve with a scoop of ice cream.  ◊

## ITALIAN FARMER'S WIFE APPLE CAKE

*How can you pass up a recipe with a name like this? I first learned about this cake from Italian cook and writer Marcella Hazan. The idea is that it is fast and not fancy, using readily available ingredients. Sweet apples to try with this recipe include McIntosh, Connell Red, and Fireside.* **SERVES 8**

..........................

  2 large eggs

 ¼ cup whole milk

  1 cup granulated sugar

pinch salt

  1 teaspoon almond extract

 ½ teaspoon ground cinnamon

1½ cups unbleached all-purpose flour

  2 pounds sweet apples (see head note), peeled, cored, and sliced thin

  1 tablespoon apple brandy

 ¼ cup honey

  2 tablespoons confectioners' sugar

 ¼ cup blanched almonds, toasted

..........................

Preheat oven to 375 degrees. Grease a 9-inch springform pan. Use a mixer to beat the eggs and milk. Add the sugar, salt, almond extract, and cinnamon and continue to beat for about 1 minute. With the mixer on low, add the flour, mixing well to combine. In a large bowl, stir together the apples with brandy and honey. Using a wooden spoon or rubber spatula, gently stir the apples into the batter, coating evenly. Pour the batter into the prepared pan, place pan on a baking sheet, and bake for approximately 45–50 minutes, until a wooden pick inserted in the center comes out clean. Let cool for about 20 minutes. Loosen cake from the bottom of the pan and transfer to a serving plate. Sprinkle with confectioners' sugar and almonds. ◇

# GINGER APPLESAUCE CAKE

*The crystallized ginger and Demerara sugar give this quick dessert a little pizzazz. Dress it up even more with a dollop of fresh whipped cream and an additional sprinkle of crystallized ginger on top.* **SERVES 12**

1½ cups unbleached all-purpose flour

1 teaspoon baking soda

½ teaspoon salt

⅔ cup raw or Demerara or natural cane sugar, plus 1 tablespoon for garnish

½ teaspoon ground ginger

¼ teaspoon ground cardamom

1 large egg, lightly beaten

8 tablespoons (1 stick) unsalted butter, melted and cooled

1½ cups Not-So-Old-Fashioned Applesauce (page 18)

1 tablespoon grated fresh ginger

1 teaspoon vanilla

1 crisp, tart apple (Zestar or SweeTango), cored and chopped

½ cup chopped walnuts

2 tablespoons chopped crystallized ginger

Preheat oven to 350 degrees. Grease an 8x8–inch baking dish. In a medium bowl, whisk together the flour, baking soda, and salt. Set aside. In a large bowl, whisk together the ⅔ cup sugar, ground ginger, and cardamom. Set aside 2 tablespoons of this mixture for the topping. Whisk the egg into the remaining sugar mixture. Slowly add the butter, applesauce, grated ginger, and vanilla. Stir in the flour mixture until blended and moist. Gently stir in the apple and walnuts. Pour batter into prepared pan and smooth top with a spatula. Sprinkle with the reserved sugar-spice mixture and crystallized ginger. Bake for 35 to 40 minutes, until a wooden pick inserted in the center comes out clean. Sprinkle with remaining tablespoon of sugar. Cool on a wire rack. ◊

# HARD CIDER SOFT ROLLED APPLE CAKE

*I like to call this cake the "ooey gooey soft rolled cake." It's like a combination of a cinnamon roll and an apple upside-down cake.* **SERVES 8**

........................

1 (.25-ounce) package active dry yeast

1 cup whole milk, warmed to 95 degrees

10 tablespoons (1¼ sticks) softened butter, divided

½ cup granulated sugar

5 large egg yolks

1 teaspoon vanilla

zest of 1 lemon

4 cups unbleached all-purpose flour

2 teaspoons salt

1 tablespoon cinnamon

4 tablespoons raw or Demerara or natural cane sugar, divided

4 apples: 2 peeled, cored, and minced, and 2 peeled, cored, and cut into wedges

¼ cup hard cider

........................

Preheat oven to 350 degrees. In a small bowl, combine the yeast with the warm milk, stirring to dissolve yeast. Set aside. Use a stand mixer fitted with the paddle attachment to beat 8 tablespoons butter with granulated sugar until fluffy. Add egg yolks, one at a time, mixing just until combined. Add the vanilla and lemon zest, and mix in the yeast and milk. In a medium bowl, whisk together the flour and salt. With the mixer running on low speed, gradually add the flour. Mix for 4 minutes on medium speed. Cover and set aside until the dough doubles in size, about 1 hour.

Meanwhile, set a skillet over medium heat. Melt remaining 2 tablespoons butter and stir in cinnamon and 2 tablespoons Demerara sugar. Add the minced apples and cook, stirring occasionally, until soft, about 20 minutes. Pour in the hard cider and cook to reduce the liquid, scraping the bottom of the pan to remove any browned bits. Remove from heat and set aside.

On a lightly floured work surface, roll out dough to a ½ inch–thick rectangle. Spread the minced apple mixture on top of the dough and roll up lengthwise. Brush a 10-inch cake pan with butter and sprinkle with remaining 2 tablespoons Demerara sugar. Layer the apple wedges in the bottom of the pan. Set the rolled dough on top of the apple wedges. Cover and let rise again until double in size, about 30 minutes. Bake for about 50 minutes, until golden. Cool for about 10 minutes, then unmold onto cake plate. ◊

## GINGER CHEESECAKE WITH APPLE TOPPING

*A luscious cheesecake is perfect for special occasions because it has to be made ahead and it is big enough for a group. Despite the name, it is not a cake but actually a custard. Be careful to avoid overbaking a cheesecake. It should be quite jiggly in the center. Underbake it a bit to protect against the dreaded cracking. If this cake still cracks, worry not: just cover it with an abundant layer of syrupy apples.* **SERVES 12**

**CRUST**

2  cups finely ground Swedish ginger cookies or gingersnaps

3  tablespoons sugar

7  tablespoons unsalted butter, melted and cooled

**FILLING**

4  (8-ounce) packages cream cheese, at room temperature

2  tablespoons unbleached all-purpose flour

pinch salt

1¼  cups sugar

1  tablespoon vanilla

2  tablespoons finely chopped crystallized ginger

4  large eggs, at room temperature

**TOPPING**

2  tablespoons butter

½  cup sugar

3  apples, peeled, cored, and sliced

1  tablespoon Apple Spice Blend (page 15)

2  tablespoons chopped crystallized ginger

Preheat oven to 375 degrees and set a rack in the middle position. In a medium bowl, stir together the cookie crumbs and sugar. Stir in the melted butter until the crumbs are evenly moist and clump together slightly. Transfer mixture to a 9-inch springform pan and use your fingers or a measuring cup to press evenly onto the bottom and about 2 inches up the sides of the pan. Bake until the crust is fragrant and slightly darkened, 9 to 12 minutes. Let cool on a rack. Reduce oven temperature to 300 degrees.

For the filling, use a stand mixer fitted with the paddle attachment to beat the cream cheese, flour, and salt on medium speed, scraping down the sides of the bowl and the paddle several times, until very smooth and fluffy, about 5 minutes. Add the sugar and continue beating until well blended and smooth. Add the vanilla and crystallized ginger and beat until blended, about 30 seconds. Add the eggs, one at a time, beating just until blended. Pour the filling into the cooled crust and smooth the top. Bake for about 55 minutes, until the edges are set and the center still jiggles. Cool to room temperature, then cover and refrigerate until well chilled, at least 8 hours and up to 3 days.

For the topping, in a medium saucepan, melt the butter and add the sugar, stirring until it dissolves. Stir in the apples and spice blend. Cook until the apples are tender and a syrup forms. Remove from heat and set aside.

Run a knife along the edge of the springform pan. Unclasp and remove the ring, then run a long, thin metal spatula under the bottom crust. Carefully slide the cake onto a flat serving plate. Before serving, slather the cheesecake with the apple topping and sprinkle with crystallized ginger. ◇

## DEEP DISH ALL-MIDWESTERN APPLE PIE

*Is any other iconic dessert more anticipated and loved than fall's first apple pie? When a slice of apple pie topped with a slab of Cheddar cheese is placed in front of my father-in-law, Ed, he always smiles and recites with delight, "A slice of pie without the cheese is like a kiss without the squeeze!" While there are surely as many family apple pie recipes as there are apple varieties, I would be remiss if I didn't include at least one as a tribute. It takes two pounds of apples to make a standard apple pie. This spectacular deep-dish version will take four pounds. Haralson is a wonderful choice for pie because of its sweetness and firm texture.* **SERVES 8**

pastry for 2-crust pie

4 pounds apples (see head note), peeled, cored, and sliced

juice of 1 lemon

½ cup raw or natural cane sugar

2 teaspoons Apple Spice Blend (page 15)

¼ cup unbleached all-purpose flour

¼ teaspoon salt

¼ cup honey

4 tablespoons (½ stick) butter

8 slices aged Cheddar (Widmer's two-year)

Preheat oven to 400 degrees. Fit one crust into a 9-inch deep-dish pie pan. In a large bowl, mix together apples and lemon juice. In a small bowl, stir together sugar, spice blend, flour, and salt. Toss sugar mixture with apples. Pour into prepared pie shell. Drizzle with honey and dot with butter. Place second pie crust on top and crimp the edges. Cut slits in top. Place on a cookie sheet. Bake for 15 minutes, then reduce heat to 350 degrees. Bake for another 60 minutes, until golden brown. If the top is browning too quickly, gently cover with aluminum foil. Serve topped with Cheddar cheese.

*Tip:* To always have great apples "on the ready" for when you are asked to bring your famous apple pie, follow this advice from Donna at Remick's Orchard in Anoka, Minnesota. Rinse, peel, core, and slice apples. In a large bowl, stir together apples with sugar, spice blend, flour, and salt. Spoon into a zip-top freezer bag and store flat in the freezer. Thaw for a few hours at room temperature or overnight in the refrigerator before filling the pie shell.  ◇

# BEVERAGES

**A**pple juice in all its adaptations proved an important component to settling the New World. Where water was believed to be unsafe, apple juice became a liquid necessary for survival. Most apples were not suitable for eating out of hand, so they were pressed and their juice preserved through fermentation and distillation. Thus, the juice of apples was also an essential resource for entertainment, which is still true today. Apple beverages, whether homemade or store bought, whether mulled with or without alcohol, provide delicious libations for fall and winter entertaining.

## APPLE TISANE (FRESH APPLE TEA)

*A tisane is an infusion of fruits, herbs, or spices. Since there are no tea leaves involved, it isn't really a tea. Whenever you are baking with apples and the recipe calls for peeling, you get a bonus: free do-it-yourself herbal tea or, more correctly, tisane. This simple, sweet, and flavorful preparation will make the whole house smell wonderful.*

Place the reserved peelings from 2 apples of any variety in a medium saucepan and cover with water. Bring to a simmer over medium heat, and let simmer for about 20 minutes. Strain liquid into your favorite teacup, discarding the solids. For best flavor, serve immediately. A cinnamon stick is an optional accompaniment. ◇

## Fresh Apple Cider

As soon as the weather turns crisp and the leaves begin to change color, something triggers a craving for apple cider. Enjoying fresh cider in the autumn is—dare I say it?—as American as apple pie. Coming through the door and getting a whiff of mulled cider whispers comfort to my kids, and I was always sure to have a kettle on the stove when they returned home from various fall and winter activities.

Cider is unfiltered, unfermented fresh apple juice, and it's easy to make at home without any fancy equipment. If you're inclined to produce many gallons of cider, consider purchasing a juicer. A few new ones on the market offer incredible, fast, and easy results. "Seconds" or small apples are perfect for cider as long as they have good flavor, and a mixture of tart and sweet is best. La Crescent and Honeycrisp work well together, or try Haralson and Connell Red. **MAKES 1 GALLON**

............................

36 medium apples (about 12 pounds)

............................

Rinse and core the apples. Remove any bruises. Cut into quarters. Puree the apples in a food processor or blender. Line a colander with a large double square of cheesecloth and place over a large saucepan or soup pot. Scoop the apple puree into the colander. Gather up the corners of the cheesecloth and twist to squeeze juice from pulp. Repeat several times. When you have captured all the juice you can, set aside the pulp (see below), place saucepan over medium-high heat, and heat liquid to a minimum of 165 degrees and not more than 185 degrees, measuring with a food thermometer. It will taste best if you don't let it boil, but you need to bring it to temperature to kill any bacteria. Cider will keep in the refrigerator for up to 5 days. It can also be frozen for 6 months. Warm the cider on the stove with ¼ cup mulling spices (page 16) per half gallon and serve hot.

Warm the pulp over medium heat and season with 1 tablespoon Apple Spice Blend (page 15) and ¼ cup honey for a quick applesauce. ◊

## HARD CIDER

Hard cider, or fermented apple juice, comes in many varieties, from dry to sweet, just like wine. Hard cider can appear cloudy or clear, and its color can range from amber to brown. Some varieties are sparkling and some are still. Only in the United States do we refer to apple juice without fermentation as cider and cider with fermentation (that is, alcohol) as *hard cider*. To make hard cider at home, you need a few simple tools, apple juice, yeast, and time. For complete home brewing instructions and equipment, visit www.midwestsupplies.com.

The most important beverage in the British colonies was hard cider. Water was often unsafe for drinking, and thus a whole industry surrounding cider was created. Apple seeds were brought from England by the early colonists, and New England has been famous for apples— and cider—ever since.

In recent years, hard cider has been experiencing a rebirth in popularity. Bars and pubs may offer several varieties on tap. It can also be used as an ingredient for making a lovely reduction pan sauce. Wherever apples are grown, hard cider is produced. England, Poland, and Germany all tout distinctive hard ciders, but some of the finest in the world are found in the Normandy region of France. More locally, Sociable Cider Werks crafts fine ciders in Minneapolis using fresh, local apples. Owners Jim and Wade remind us that hard cider should be enjoyed like a great draft beer. For more information, visit their website: www.sociablecider.com.

## APPLE BRANDY VERSUS APPLEJACK

A step up from hard cider, apple brandy is made from mashed apples twice distilled and aged in barrels. The most respected apple brandy is the famous Calvados, from the Normandy region of France. The oldest known distillery for Calvados dates back to 1554 and was owned by Lord de Gouberville. The guild for cider distillation was formed about fifty years later, in 1606. Historical records show that apple brandy was an important supply for the armed services from the American Revolutionary War through World War I. George Washington specifically ordered it as a ration for his soldiers. Until recently, apple brandy in the United States consisted of one option, Laird's AppleJack, produced in Scobeyville, New Jersey, since 1780. During Prohibition, Laird and Company even had a license to produce applejack for medicinal purposes. Now, craft distilleries are booming, and throughout the Midwest there are many fine handmade, small-batch apple brandies to choose from.

Apple brandy can be quite sophisticated, with many nuances of flavors and aromas from being aged in oak barrels. The finer apple brandies are probably best enjoyed in a snifter straight, like a fine cognac. Applejack, which is not usually aged in wood, is the less-refined cousin. Often fortified with other spirits, it is also called apple whiskey and is delightful when used in cocktails.

Here are a few apple brandies to look for at the liquor store:

- Calvados, Normandy, aged in oak for two years
- Laird & Company, Scobeyville, New Jersey
- Cedar Ridge Vineyards, Swisher, Iowa
- Yahara Bay Distillers, Madison, Wisconsin
- Koval Distillery, Chicago, Illinois

## GINGER APPLETINI

*The appletini conjures an image of a cloyingly sweet cocktail made with artificial green color and flavor, but this well-balanced rendition uses fresh ginger among other natural ingredients for a refined drink.* **SERVES 4**

4 cups Fresh Apple Cider (page 160)

2 inches fresh ginger, peeled and minced

½ cup vodka

1 large pasteurized egg white

2 cups club soda

1 apple, sliced in rounds

Pour cider into a heavy-bottomed saucepan, stir in ginger, and bring to a simmer over medium-high heat. Reduce heat and simmer for 15 minutes. Pour apple-ginger mixture through a fine-mesh strainer. Set aside liquid to cool; discard solids.

Fill 4 cocktail glasses and a cocktail shaker with ice. To the shaker, add vodka, 1 cup apple-ginger cider, and egg white. Shake vigorously for 30 seconds. Empty ice from cocktail glasses, and divide liquid among the chilled glasses. Top off each with a spritz of club soda. Garnish with an apple slice. ◇

## CANDY APPLE FIZZ

*The mention of* candy apple *no doubt conjures up a tray of bright-red, shiny apples at the county fair. This whimsically named cocktail is more sophisticated and fortunately is not "Candy Apple Red," but it just might make you feel like a kid again.* **SERVES 1**

2 ounces applejack

1 ounce Fresh Apple Cider (page 160)

½ teaspoon grenadine (see tip)

¼ cinnamon stick, crushed

splash sparkling apple juice

4 slices candied apple (page 25)

Fill a cocktail shaker halfway with ice and add applejack, cider, grenadine, and crushed cinnamon stick. Shake vigorously for 30 seconds. Strain into a lowball glass over a few ice cubes or straight up in a martini glass. Add a splash of sparkling apple juice and garnish with a candied apple slice.

*Tip:* For a more refined twist, substitute Montmorency cherry concentrate for grenadine syrup. ◊

# Hot Spiced Apple Rum

*Wonderful after any favorite outdoor activities, this beverage can be enjoyed all through the fall and winter. For a perfect pairing, sip in front of a bonfire or a roaring fireplace with a platter of Brie with Apple Chutney (page 39).*

**SERVES 4**

1 orange

4 cups Fresh Apple Cider (page 160)

¼ teaspoon ground ancho chile

½ teaspoon freeze-dried or ground ginger

4 cinnamon sticks

4 whole cloves

6 ounces spiced rum, divided

Use a paring knife or a fruit peeler to remove peel from the orange in strips, being careful to leave behind the bitter white pith. In a medium saucepan stir together the orange peel, cider, ancho chile, ginger, cinnamon sticks, and cloves. Bring to a simmer over medium heat and let simmer for 15 minutes. Pour 1½ ounces rum into each of 4 mugs. Ladle the spiced cider into each mug, and garnish with a cinnamon stick and an orange peel from the pot.  ◊

## Super Power Smoothie

*A super power smoothie in a book about apples? Of course! As a nutrient-dense superfood, the apple is noted for its many nutritional benefits, especially for being high in fiber and antioxidants. Although one among many ingredients, here it is the star of the show. Without the apple's natural sweetness, this smoothie would not be nearly so delectable. Easy to make, this highly nutritious beverage will be a favorite for breakfast or a snack.*

**SERVES 2**

- 1 cup tightly packed kale leaves
- ½ cup Fresh Apple Cider (page 160)
- 2 medium apples, cored and chopped
- 3 ice cubes
- 1 tablespoon lemon juice
- 1 tablespoon minced fresh ginger
- 1 tablespoon ground flaxseed
- 1 teaspoon cinnamon
- 1 rib celery, sliced
- ½ medium sweet onion, chopped
- 1 cup fresh parsley

Place all ingredients in a blender and process until smooth. Divide into 2 glasses to serve.  ◇

# INDEX